THE AUSTRALIAN Women's Weekly

DIABETES

CONTENTS

·····································

DISCLAIMER The following information provides basic guidelines to healthy eating for people with diabetes. Please check with your doctor, dietitian or diabetes educator as to the suitability of this information for your diabetes management.

A life-changing challenge

Diabetes is the fastest growing chronic disease in Australia. Over a million Australians have been diagnosed and another 280 develop diabetes every day. Two million Australians are thought to have pre-diabetes, putting them at risk of developing type 2 diabetes in the future. However, over half these cases could be prevented with the right dietary and lifestyle changes; for those living with diabetes, these changes are essential in helping you to manage the disease.

Understanding Diabetes

Diabetes is a chronic condition, meaning that once diagnosed it is something you have to manage your whole life. Fortunately we now know much more about how to do that effectively so you can go on to live a healthy long life. This book is intended to help you do just that.

Diabetes is a condition where the body fails to produce enough of the hormone insulin, or the insulin it produces is not working as it should. Insulin's principal job is to 'unlock' cells, allowing them to take up glucose from the blood and into the cell, where it is used as fuel to produce energy for the body. Without enough insulin, the glucose levels in the blood rise, and cannot be used for energy production.

A high level of glucose in the blood is called hyperglycaemia. Over time, if this goes unchecked, it is extremely damaging to blood vessels around the body, particularly the smaller vessels in the eyes, kidneys and extremities (arms and legs). People living with diabetes are also at more risk of heart (cardiovascular) disease. For these reasons it's imperative for those living with diabetes to carefully manage the disease to lower their risk of developing complications.

TYPES OF DIABETES

Type 1 Diabetes

Type 1 and type 2 diabetes are very different diseases. Type 1 diabetes is an autoimmune disease, where the body's own immune system destroys the cells in the pancreas that produce insulin. The exact cause is not known, but it is thought that in those genetically predisposed, a virus may trigger the immune response. It is not caused by bad diet or any other lifestyle factor.

Dr Joanna McMillan
Accredited Practising
Dietitian & Nutritionist
www.drjoanna.com.au

Usually type 1 diabetes is diagnosed in childhood or in young adults under the age of 40, although it can develop later in life. Without insulin, the body has to burn fat alone, and this results in the accumulation of chemical substances in the blood called ketones. If too many ketones build up in the blood it leads to a condition called ketoacidosis. This is potentially life-threatening and must be medically treated as soon as possible (see 'Symptoms of Ketoacidosis', left). Ketoacidosis is rare in those with type 2 diabetes.

The onset of type 1 diabetes will generally develop very suddenly. Blood glucose levels are elevated and the glucose spills over into the urine.

An early symptom of type 1 diabetes is going to the bathroom frequently, yet being excessively thirsty and dehydrated. Since glucose from carbohydrates in food cannot be used for fuel, people may also experience unexplained weight loss, and may find they are always hungry. Glucose is the primary fuel for the brain, and when it cannot be used people may experience headaches, mood swings, dizziness and a 'foggy brain'.

People may also find that wounds heal slowly, their skin itches and they experience leg cramps. If these symptoms appear in you or a member of your family, see your doctor who will test for diabetes.

Daily injections of insulin and the monitoring of blood glucose levels are essential to manage type 1 diabetes. While insulin may or may not be used in type 2 diabetes, it is vital in type 1.

Following a healthy diet and lifestyle, including regular exercise, is important in all types of diabetes.

Type 2 diabetes

Type 2 diabetes is much more common than type 1, and accounts for more than 80% of all diabetes cases. It is more likely to develop as you get older but, sadly, more and more young people, including children, are being diagnosed.

If diabetes runs in your family, you are at an increased risk of developing it yourself, but in contrast to type 1, your diet and lifestyle play a major role. Being overweight, and in particular carrying too much fat around your middle, significantly increases

(continues over page)

your risk of type 2 diabetes. You are at higher risk of developing type 2 diabetes if aged over 35 and from an Aboriginal, Torres Strait Islander, Pacific Island, Indian subcontinent or Chinese cultural background. Women who have had gestational diabetes (diabetes that develops during pregnancy), or a baby born over 4.5kg (9½lbs) or polycystic ovarian syndrome are also at greater risk.

In contrast to type 1 diabetes, the pancreatic cells in type 2 diabetes continue to produce insulin. However, either not enough insulin is produced, or the insulin does not work as it should. The pancreas produces even more insulin to try to do the job. A blood test will reveal very high insulin levels, called hyperinsulinaemia.

Insulin is not just involved in blood glucose control – it also stimulates fat storage. High insulin levels can therefore lead to unexplained weight gain, a common early symptom of type 2 diabetes. Since your body is not burning fuel as it should, you may feel tired, lethargic and generally unwell. In the early days, blood glucose levels can be normal. However, eventually the cells cannot keep up with the demand for insulin and insulin levels fall, or just fail to keep blood glucose levels in check

so they rise. Blood glucose spills over into the urine and that's why doctors will usually check your urine during a checkup.

Gestational Diabetes
Gestational diabetes is a type of diabetes that develops during pregnancy in 3-8% of women. There is an increased demand for insulin during pregnancy and sometimes the pancreas fails to keep up, and gestational diabetes develops. Sometimes insulin injections are required, but often gestational diabetes can be managed by changes to diet and being more active.

Gestational diabetes goes away once the baby is born, however, women who develop gestational diabetes are more likely to develop type 2 diabetes. It is imperative to continue with a healthy diet and regular exercise program to help prevent this.

Managing Diabetes
The good news is that those living with diabetes do not need to follow a special diet, just the same healthy diet that is recommended for most of us. You don't need to buy special products or follow an extreme eating plan. However, what and how you eat does play an important role in managing the disease, so think of it as an added motivation to exercise and eat well.

SYMPTOMS OF TYPE 2 DIABETES INCLUDE
- Feeling excessively thirsty and going to the bathroom frequently
- Feeling tired, lethargic and generally unwell
- Weight gain and always feeling hungry
- Blurred vision caused by high glucose levels in the blood
- Headaches and feeling dizzy
- Itchy skin and slow healing wounds
- Leg cramps

5 Key Steps to Managing Diabetes

1. Sit less and move more. Activity and exercise help insulin to work more effectively in the body, and to get glucose into the muscle cells to be used to fuel the activity. The more time you spend sitting, the less fuel your body uses and the harder it is to control blood glucose levels. Aim for at least 30 minutes of exercise on most days. Walking is ideal. You can break this into two or three shorter walks if you prefer. In fact, a 10-15 minute walk after meals is a fantastic way to help get blood glucose back under control after eating.

2. Maintain a healthy weight. If you are overweight, losing even 5% of your body weight is enough to benefit your health and management of diabetes. So don't feel that you have failed if you don't reach your target weight. Following the healthy eating advice in this book, reducing portion sizes, ensuring you get enough sleep, regularly exercising and managing stress will help you reach and maintain a healthier weight.

3. Eat more plant food. A resounding message from nutrition research is that eating a plant-based diet is best for us all, whether or not you also eat meat. Plant food includes vegies, fruit, legumes (chickpeas, beans and lentils), wholegrains, nuts and seeds. Aim for at least 5-6 serves of different vegies and 2 serves of fruit each day.

4. Choose good fats. Gone are the days of the low-fat diet. It's now all about the right fats. Diets high in saturated fats are associated with increased insulin resistance and type 2 diabetes. Replacing saturated fat with primarily monounsaturated fats and some polyunsaturated fats can improve the action of insulin and lower your risk of cardiovascular disease. Aim to include more nuts, seeds, extra-virgin olive oil, and avocado in your daily diet. Omega-3 fats found in oily fish, such as tuna and sardines, are also terrific: aim for 2-3 serves a week.

5. Choose smart carbs. These are carbohydrate-containing foods that are digested slowly and therefore have far less impact on your blood glucose levels. They are nutrient-packed and often fibre-rich, so boost your health, and are associated with both a reduced risk of developing type 2 diabetes as well as helping with better diabetes management.

Smart carbs include whole fruit over fruit juice, reduced-fat milk and yoghurt, and minimally-processed wholegrains and legumes. At the same time, cut back on processed foods that contain refined starch and added sugars, such as soft drinks, lollies, biscuits, cakes, white bread (including bagels and crumpets), white rice and potatoes.

How much carbohydrate?

The Glycaemic Index (GI) is really a tool to assessing the quality of carbohydrate in your diet. The other key factor is how much carbohydrate you eat and when you eat it. This is different for everyone, and can vary from day to day based on activity levels.

We need insulin to survive and it has many roles in addition to controlling blood glucose levels – including stimulating muscle synthesis (which is necessary for the growth, repair and maintenance of muscle tissue) after exercise.

The more active you are, the more carbohydrate your body will use. That's why regular blood glucose monitoring is so important for those living with diabetes.

For those taking insulin it's absolutely critical you match the right amount of carbohydrate with your insulin dose – you may need to adjust your insulin dose to suit a particular meal. Not eating enough can result in a 'hypo' where blood glucose levels fall to dangerously low levels, while eating too much ('hyper') will cause your blood glucose levels to rise too high.

Your diabetes care team, including a dietitian who specialises in diabetes management, can help manage this.

Most people find a low-carb diet extremely difficult to follow long term. And, by cutting out carbohydrate-rich foods you also cut out some of the best sources of fibre, including wholegrains, legumes and whole fruit.

For those managing diabetes with diet and exercise alone, it is just as important to give consideration to your total carbohydrate intake. By consuming just the right amount, from low-GI sources, you will help your body to keep blood glucose levels in check. As a general guide, a small to moderate portion of a low-GI food at each meal is optimal to keep steady blood glucose levels over the course of the day.

Should I Follow a Low Carb Diet?

Low-carb diets are not recommended for people living with diabetes for several reasons.

1 If taking insulin (type 1) some carbohydrate is needed in your diet to balance this and ensure the body's cells get the glucose they need to function. However, if not taking insulin (type 2), eating the right carbs in the right amount can help your body to produce insulin in the right amount.

2 A low-carb diet is almost always high in protein, and there are concerns about the effect of this in those with kidney problems, including people living with diabetes, who have greater risk of kidney disease.

3 IF YOU HAVE DIABETES YOU ARE AT GREATER RISK OF CARDIOVASCULAR DISEASE. LOW-CARB DIETS TEND TO BE HIGH IN SATURATED FATS, AND A DIET HIGH IN SATURATED FATS IS NOT GOOD FOR CARDIAC HEALTH.

4 A high-saturated fat diet has been shown to increase insulin resistance. Other dietary factors also affect how cells respond to insulin. Diabetes is much more complicated than being just about carbohydrate intake. Studies of the Mediterranean-style diet, where the fat comes primarily from extra virgin olive oil, nuts, seeds and avocado, all low in saturated fats, reduces the risk of heart disease and type 2 diabetes.

5 Studies have shown that using poly- or mono- unsaturated fats instead of saturated fats improves blood cholesterol.

6 The bottom line is that there are good quality nutritious foods containing carbs and those that are nutrient-poor and high GI. Moderate your carbohydrate intake with a focus on the best quality foods, rather than cutting out carbs altogether.

7 Steps to a Low-GI Diet

1. Instead of buying bakery foods made primarily with white flour (think white bread, crumpets, scones, pikelets and so on), choose wholegrain breads with lots of grainy 'bits', stoneground wholemeal or sourdough rye, grainy or soy & linseed breads.
If you really want white bread, sourdough white bread tends to have a lower GI and there are several supermarket white breads with added fibre and a lower GI.

2. Cut back on high GI snacks including banana bread, muffins, cakes and biscuits. These foods are also high in kilojoules and low in nutrients. Instead, snack on a handful of unsalted nuts, whole fruit, yoghurt or a vegie-based smoothie.

3. Potatoes and potato products including mash and chips, tend to be high GI. Smaller salad potatoes tend to have a lower GI, making them a better choice provided you watch your portion size. Try making homemade chips with a mixture of sweet potatoes, beetroot, carrots and parsnip. Cut the vegies into wedges, drizzle or spray with extra virgin olive oil and bake in the oven for 30 minutes. Always leave the skin on for extra fibre and nutrients.
You can also make mash with canned cannellini beans, a little extra virgin olive oil and garlic. Or make a vegie mash using cauliflower, parsnip and sweet potato.

4. Use more legumes. Dried beans, chickpeas and lentils are all low GI and fantastically nutrient-rich, providing folate and other B-group vitamins, iron, zinc and magnesium. They provide good levels of protein along with low GI carbohydrates and stacks of fibre, particularly soluble fibre – the type that helps to control blood glucose levels. Add canned beans to salads, soups, casseroles, or even to bolognese sauce; mash with spices, herbs and plain yoghurt to make a dip; make hummus with canned chickpeas, or mash and turn them into patties and pop on the BBQ.

5. Watch the type and amount of rice you eat when eating out and at home. Jasmine rice (the usual rice in Thai and other Asian style cuisines), arborio rice (used in Italian risottos) and calrose rice (another popular white rice) have extremely high GI values and are not the best choices.

Instead, look for basmati, Doongara and Moolgiri rice varieties. These have much lower GI values because they have a higher proportion of the type of starch that takes longer for our bodies to break down (called amylose). If you can find the 'brown' versions of these rice varieties, you also get the extra benefits of the fibre and nutrients from the wholegrain variety. You can also try using less rice and mixing your rice with lentils or beans for a lower GI, higher protein and more filling meal.

You can also substitute rice for low GI wholegrains such as freekeh, bulgur or barley, or the pseudograin quinoa (it's actually a seed, but we eat it like a grain).

6. Select breakfast cereals carefully. Even wholegrain varieties can have high GI values as the wholegrain is so finely ground and processed that our bodies can readily access the starch and break it down easily. Look for those varieties labelled low GI, or use the international glycaemic index database (managed by Sydney University) at *www. glycemicindex.com* to find the varieties that have been tested and shown to have a low GI. Or, opt for traditional porridge oats (not instant), natural muesli or make your own muesli using oats, nuts, seeds and a little dried fruit.

7. Dairy products, including milk and yoghurt, have low GI values and are terrific choices for helping manage blood glucose levels. They are also important sources of protein and calcium, required for healthy bones. If you can't or don't want to have dairy, be careful with alternatives. Rice milk has an extremely high GI, while many other alternative 'milks' have not been tested. Soy milks, being low GI, are your best option.

Understanding GI

The glycaemic index is a fantastic tool to help you choose the best carbohydrate-containing foods.

Glycaemic just means glucose in the blood, and the GI is literally a measure of how much the food will raise your blood glucose levels compared to consuming the same amount of carbohydrate as pure glucose. Glucose is the benchmark and has a GI of 100, and all other foods are essentially a percentage of this.

Foods with a GI of:
55 or less are low GI
56-69 are moderate GI
70 or higher are high GI

Choosing low GI foods over high GI foods will help you to control your blood glucose and lower your body's demand for insulin. They have also been shown to improve blood lipid profiles (cholesterol and triglycerides) in people with both type 1 and type 2 diabetes. They can also help you to control your weight as low GI foods are more slowly digested, so they keep you fuller for longer and help you to manage your hunger and eat less over the course of the day.

What About Sugar?

A healthy diet can include a little sugar, and the same applies to those living with diabetes. However, foods with lots of added sugar and little nutritional value are not helpful.

These include lollies, confectionery, soft drinks, biscuits, cakes and desserts. Aside from their effects on blood glucose control, these foods are likely to affect both your weight and your dental health. Of course, if you wish, you can enjoy them every now and again, but take care to keep your portion size small when you do. You can make healthier versions of many of these foods yourself at home, using far less sugar, and you'll find some terrific options in this book. Other foods that are nutritious, but have a little sugar added for palatability, are perfectly acceptable as part of an overall healthy eating plan.

Wholegrain breakfast cereals, fruit yoghurts and homemade fruit-based desserts, are all good examples. Overall, look to include foods that naturally contain sugar and offer lots of nutrition, fruit being the best example. Here, the sugar is bound up within the plant cell walls, so the body has to work to get the sugar out and absorbed for use. Fibre, vitamins, minerals and beneficial plant compounds, such as antioxidants, are also present in fruits, making such foods valuable to us. This is not the same thing as a fruit-flavoured lolly!

A Healthy Eating Plan for Diabetes in a Nutshell

1 Eat more vegies: aim for at least 5-6 serves of different vegies a day, plus 2 pieces of fruit. Aim to fill half your plate with non-starchy vegies at two of your daily meals.

2 Choose low GI wholegrains, legumes and starchy vegetables, including a small serve at each meal to help manage blood glucose levels over the course of the day.

4 CHOOSE FOODS THAT ARE RICH IN POLY- AND MONO- UNSATURATED (GOOD) FATS EVERY DAY INCLUDING EXTRA VIRGIN OLIVE OIL, UNSALTED NUTS, SEEDS AND AVOCADO.

3 Include a protein-rich food at each meal. Choose from lean red meat, poultry, game meats, fish, seafood, eggs, dairy products, tofu or legumes. These foods help to control appetite and blood glucose, and can assist with weight control.

5 Choose oily fish, rich in omega-3 fats, 2-3 times a week. These have an anti-inflammatory effect in the body, and are good for both brain and heart health. Examples include salmon, trout, tuna, sardines, herring and mackerel.

7 Limit foods that are high in saturated fat, added sugars and refined starch (high GI, highly processed grain foods).

6 EAT SMALL REGULAR MEALS SPREAD OVER THE COURSE OF THE DAY. THIS HELPS MANAGE BOTH YOUR APPETITE AND YOUR BLOOD GLUCOSE LEVELS.

What's on a Plate

The key to portion control is to downsize some foods and increase others to achieve a balanced plate. An easy way to judge this is to divide your plate into quarters. Roughly, one quarter should be carbohydrates, another quarter should be protein and two quarters should be non-starchy vegetables. Never pile food higher than a flat deck of cards. The diameter of the inside rim of the plate is 20cm (8 inches).

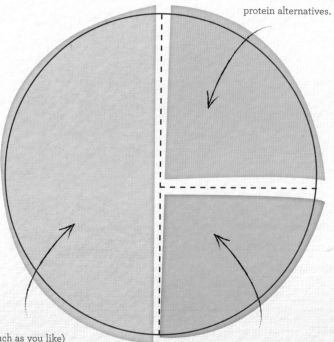

LEAN PROTEIN
65-100g chicken breast; fish fillet; lean steak; or protein alternatives.

FREE VEGETABLES/SALAD (eat as much as you like)
Lettuce, broccoli, broccolini, asparagus, celery, green beans, beetroot, tomatoes, cabbage, capsicum, cauliflower, cucumber, brussels sprouts, mushrooms, onion, leeks, spinach, squash, leafy salad mixes, zucchini, radish.

HIGH-FIBRE/LOWER-GI CARBOHYDRATE
Steamed couscous; pasta or rice (basmati or doongara); wholegrain bread; baked kumara (orange sweet potato); fresh corn; or legumes.

Visual Reminder USING YOUR HAND – PER SERVING

PALM OF HAND
Portion of cooked fish, lean meat or skinless chicken.

FIST
Approximately 1 cup fresh fruit; 1 serving of low-fat milk or yoghurt.

THREE MIDDLE FINGERS TOGETHER
Size of potato.

LENGTH OF THUMB
Amount of avocado, nuts or seeds.

TIP OF THUMB
Amount of peanut butter/vegemite/jam. Amount of unsaturated oil and margarine.

CENTRE OF CUPPED PALM
(approximately 50c piece)
Amount of unsalted nuts and reduced-fat cheese.

7-day Menu Planner

DAY	BREAKFAST	SNACK	LUNCH	SNACK	DINNER	DESSERT	TOTAL DAILY INTAKE
MONDAY	Roasted field mushrooms with garlic, spinach and ricotta (page 16)	1 small banana	Ginger and chilli chicken rice paper rolls (page 55)	½ cup mixed berries with 1 small (100g) tub low-fat fruit yoghurt	Lamb cutlets with smashed potatoes and brussels sprouts salad (page 74)	Tropical jelly with coconut yoghurt (page 98)	39.4g total fat (11.6g saturated fat); 6473kJ (1546 cal); 158.1g carbohydrate; 113.7g protein; 37.7g fibre; 708mg sodium
TUESDAY	Poached egg and avocado bruschetta (page 26)	½ cup fresh strawberries	Chai roasted pumpkin soup with honey walnuts (page 63)	1 small pear	Barbecued squid with lemon cracked wheat risotto (page 66)	Nectarine and almond tarte tartin (page 104)	55.5g total fat (11g saturated fat); 5889kJ (14.6 cal); 151.9g carbohydrate; 58.1g protein; 34.6g fibre; 1243mg sodium
WEDNESDAY	Berry semolina porridge (page 29)	1 apple plus 1 small (100g) tub low fat fruit yoghurt	Mixed mushroom trencher with herb salad (page 59)	2 kiwi fruit	Korean beef lettuce cups with pickled vegetables (page 69)	Very berry ice-cream sandwiches (page 106)	42.8g total fat (9.4g saturated fat); 6997kJ (1672 cal); 209.5g carbohydrate; 92.9g protein; 35.4g fibre; 1203mg sodium
THURSDAY	Grilled fruit salad with coconut yoghurt (page 23)	1 orange	Lime and coriander beef salad (page 43)	1 small (100g) tub low-fat fruit yoghurt	Kaffir lime and red curry fish parcels (page 77)	Rhubarb and vanilla baked custard (page 101)	30g total fat (9.1g saturated fat); 5665kJ (1353 cal); 147.9g carbohydrate; 105.3g protein; 29.9g fibre; 1039mg sodium
FRIDAY	Scrambled egg, smashed avocado and bean breakfast wrap (page 21)	1 apple	Rocket, chicken and date salad (page 38)	½ cup blueberries	Pork and sage meatballs with cabbage and pear (page 81)	Roasted pears with cinnamon labneh (page 101)	52.9g total fat (13.7g saturated fat); 6813kJ (1628 cal); 175.2g carbohydrate; 91.7g protein; 45.9g fibre; 741mg sodium
SATURDAY	Pea fritters with avocado goat's cheese (page 29)	1 small banana	Spiced vegetable, chickpea and ricotta salad (page 46)	2 kiwi fruit	Salmon with green papaya and pink grapefruit salad (page 85)	Orange and pomegranate steamed puddings (page 104)	73g total fat (18.2g saturated fat); 7519kJ (1796 cal); 183.4g carbohydrate; 82.8g protein; 37.2g fibre; 1265mg sodium
SUNDAY	Baked bean and tomato pots with rosemary sourdough crumble (page 22)	1 pear	Thai prawn burger (page 56)	½ cup strawberries with 1 small (100g) tub low-fat fruit yoghurt	Baked chicken with maple parsnips (page 88)	Caramel swirl ice-cream sandwiches (page 107)	44.3g total fat (8.1g saturated fat); 5796kJ (1385 cal); 150.2g carbohydrate; 81.5g protein; 42.4g fibre; 1288g sodium

This menu planner is a guide only. It is important that you eat a balanced diet in order to get all the nutrients your body requires.

breakfast

roasted field mushrooms with garlic, spinach and ricotta

PREP + COOK TIME 40 MINUTES • SERVES 2

4 medium portobello field mushrooms (400g), trimmed

275g (9 ounces) baby truss tomatoes

rice bran oil spray

2 cloves garlic, crushed

1 tablespoon balsamic vinegar

1 teaspoon extra virgin olive oil

12 sprigs fresh thyme

50g (1½ ounces) baby spinach leaves

¼ cup (25g) low-fat ricotta cheese

3 slices multigrain bread (135g), toasted

1 Preheat oven to 200°C/400°F. Line a large baking dish with baking paper.
2 Place mushrooms and tomato in baking dish. Spray lightly with oil. Season with pepper.
3 Combine garlic, vinegar and olive oil in a small bowl; drizzle over mushrooms, sprinkle mushrooms with thyme. Cover pan loosely with baking paper. Bake for 20 minutes.
4 Discard top baking paper. Tuck spinach leaves under mushrooms and tomato. Dollop mushrooms with ricotta. Bake, uncovered, for 5 minutes or until vegetables are tender. Serve with toast.

If portobello mushrooms are unavailable use large field mushrooms.

indian-style tomatoes and eggs

PREP + COOK TIME 45 MINUTES • SERVES 2

2 teaspoons rice bran oil

1 small brown onion (80g), chopped finely

1 long fresh red chilli, seeded, chopped finely

2 cloves garlic, crushed

½ teaspoon each brown mustard seeds and cumin seeds

2 tablespoons fresh curry leaves

400g (12½ ounces) grape tomatoes, halved

4 small eggs

1 wholemeal lebanese bread (80g)

¼ cup firmly packed fresh mint leaves

1 Heat oil in a large non-stick pan over medium-low heat; cook onion and chilli, covered, for 5 minutes, stirring occasionally, or until onion is soft. Add garlic, seeds and curry leaves; cook, stirring, for 1 minute or until fragrant. Add tomato; cook, stirring, for 5 minutes or until softened. Season with pepper.

2 Meanwhile, half fill a large shallow frying pan with water; bring to the boil. Break 1 egg into a cup then slide into pan; repeat with remaining eggs. When all eggs are in the pan, allow water to return to the boil. Cover pan, turn off heat; stand for 3 minutes or until a light film of egg white sets over yolks.

3 Using a slotted spoon remove eggs, one at a time, from pan; drain on kitchen paper, cover to keep warm.

4 Heat a grill pan (or grill or barbecue) over high heat; cook bread for 1 minute each side or until lightly charred. Cut toast into wedges.

5 Divide tomato mixture between plates; top with eggs, sprinkle with mint. Serve with toast.

If fresh curry leaves aren't available use dried leaves.

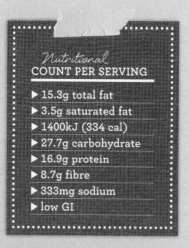

Nutritional
COUNT PER SERVING

▶ 15.3g total fat

▶ 3.5g saturated fat

▶ 1400kJ (334 cal)

▶ 27.7g carbohydrate

▶ 16.9g protein

▶ 8.7g fibre

▶ 333mg sodium

▶ low GI

Test Kitchen
NOTES

We used two mountain bread wraps for each serve, this helps the wrap stay together as one wrap tends to be fragile. We used ½ x 400g (12½ ounce) can salt-reduced kidney beans for this recipe. Omit the chilli or remove the seeds, if you like.

scrambled egg, smashed avocado and bean breakfast wrap

PREP + COOK TIME 20 MINUTES • SERVES 2

1 small avocado (100g)

2 teaspoons lime juice

2 teaspoons finely grated lime rind

130g (4 ounces) rinsed, drained canned kidney beans

1 medium tomato (150g), chopped finely

½ small red onion (50g), sliced thinly

1 long fresh green chilli, sliced thinly

¼ cup loosely packed fresh coriander leaves (cilantro)

2 eggs

2 egg whites

1 tablespoon skim milk

1 tablespoon coarsely chopped fresh coriander (cilantro) leaves

1 teaspoon rice bran oil

4 rye mountain bread wraps (100g)

1 Mash avocado, juice and half the rind roughly in a small bowl with a fork. Season with pepper.

2 Combine kidney beans, tomato, onion, chilli, coriander leaves and remaining rind in a small bowl. Season with black pepper.

3 Whisk eggs, egg whites, milk and chopped coriander in a small bowl until combined.

4 Heat oil in a medium non-stick frying pan over medium-low heat; cook egg mixture, stirring gently, for 2 minutes or until just set.

5 Place two wraps together. Spread wrap with half the avocado mixture; top with half the bean mixture and half the scrambled egg. Roll up to form a wrap; cut in half. Repeat with remaining wraps.

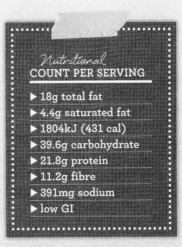

Nutritional
COUNT PER SERVING

▶ 18g total fat

▶ 4.4g saturated fat

▶ 1804kJ (431 cal)

▶ 39.6g carbohydrate

▶ 21.8g protein

▶ 11.2g fibre

▶ 391mg sodium

▶ low GI

baked beans and tomato pots with rosemary sourdough crumble

PREP + COOK TIME 2½ HOURS (+ STANDING) • SERVES 2

Nutritional
COUNT PER SERVING

▶ 13.1g total fat
▶ 1.9g saturated fat
▶ 1459kJ (349 cal)
▶ 30.3g carbohydrate
▶ 21.5g protein
▶ 16.1g fibre
▶ 310mg sodium
▶ low GI

Start this recipe the day before.

½ cup (100g) dried cannellini beans

rice bran oil spray

1 medium brown onion (150g), chopped finely

2 cloves garlic, crushed

1½ teaspoons chopped fresh rosemary

1 teaspoon ground cumin

pinch chilli flakes

400g (12½ ounces) canned cherry tomatoes in juice

1 cup (250ml) water

60g (2 ounces) white sourdough bread, torn roughly

1 tablespoon small fresh rosemary sprigs

1 Cover beans in a large bowl with cold water; stand 8 hours or overnight. Drain.
2 Cook beans in a large saucepan of boiling water for 45 minutes or until tender. Drain.
3 Preheat oven to 200°C/400°F.
4 Spray a medium non-stick frying pan with oil, heat over low heat; cook onion, stirring, for 10 minutes or until softened. Add garlic, rosemary, cumin and chilli; cook, stirring, for 1 minute or until fragrant. Add tomatoes, the water and beans, bring to the boil; reduce heat, simmer, uncovered, for 10 minutes or until thickened slightly. Season with pepper.
5 Spoon mixture into 2 x 1½-cup (375ml) ovenproof dishes; place on a baking tray. Top mixture with torn bread and rosemary sprigs. Spray with oil.
6 Bake for 15 minutes or until browned and bubbling.

You can use canned cannellini beans, but be aware that the sodium content of your meal will increase.

grilled fruit salad with coconut yoghurt

1 medium pear (230g), cored, cut into eight wedges

4 medium figs (240g), halved lengthways

1 medium blood orange (240g), peeled, cut into 1cm (½-inch) thick slices

⅓ cup (95g) coconut yoghurt

3 teaspoons sunflower seeds, toasted

1 Cook pear on a heated lightly oiled grill plate (or grill or barbecue), over medium-high heat, for 4 minutes each side or until slightly tender and charred.
2 Add figs halfway through cooking time; cook for 2 minutes each side until figs are tender and charred.
3 Combine grilled fruit with orange in serving bowls; top with yoghurt and sunflower seeds.

Test Kitchen
NOTES

To cook figs, place a small sheet of baking paper on the grill plate to prevent the figs from sticking. You could also eat this fruit salad fresh without grilling the fruit, for a breakfast on-the-go. Pure coconut yoghurt is dairy-free and is available from health food stores.

Nutritional
COUNT PER SERVING

▶ 4g total fat
▶ 2.1g saturated fat
▶ 953kJ (228 cal)
▶ 36.8g carbohydrate
▶ 5.6g protein
▶ 10g fibre
▶ 37mg sodium
▶ low GI

smokey shakshuka

½ teaspoon loosely packed saffron

½ cup (125ml) water

½ teaspoon cumin seeds

3 teaspoons rice bran oil

1 small brown onion (80g), sliced thinly

2 cloves garlic, crushed

1 small red capsicum (150g), sliced thinly

100g (3 ounces) extra lean minced (ground) beef

2 tablespoons coarsely chopped fresh flat-leaf parsley

5 medium vine-ripened tomatoes (750g), chopped coarsely

½ chipotle chilli in adobo sauce, chopped finely

1 teaspoon smoked paprika

100g (3 ounces) baby spinach leaves

1 wholemeal pitta (85g), torn crossways

2 small eggs

1 Combine saffron and the water in a small jug.

2 Toast cumin seeds in a large deep dry frying pan over medium heat for 1 minute or until fragrant, remove from pan.

3 Heat 2 teaspoons of the oil in same pan; cook onion, garlic, capsicum and beef, stirring, for 5 minutes or until beef is browned and vegetables are tender.

4 Add saffron mixture, cumin, parsley, tomato, chilli and paprika to pan; bring to the boil. Reduce heat; simmer, uncovered, stirring occasionally, for 10 minutes or until mixture has thickened slightly. (If the mixture sticks to the pan while cooking, add 1 tablespoon of water to the pan to help stop the ingredients sticking.) Stir through half the spinach. Season with pepper to taste.

5 Meanwhile, heat a grill pan (or grill or barbecue) over medium heat. Rub pitta with remaining oil on both sides; cook for 1 minute each side or until charred. Remove from pan; cover to keep warm.

6 Make two indents in the hot tomato mixture with the back of a spoon. Break 1 egg into a cup, slide into indent. Repeat with remaining egg. Reduce heat to low; cook, covered, for 4 minutes or until egg whites are set.

7 Top with remaining spinach, serve with pitta.

Test Kitchen NOTES

Chipotle chilli with adobo sauce can be found in most good grocers and delicatessens. You can up the chilli for a little more heat or you can substitute chipotle chilli with 1 fresh long red chilli or ½ teaspoon dried chilli flakes if you prefer.
You can prepare the recipe the day before up to the end of step 4; just before serving, reheat and continue from step 5.

poached egg and avocado bruschetta

PREP + COOK TIME 20 MINUTES • SERVES 2

1 teaspoon rice bran oil

2 teaspoons lemon juice

¼ teaspoon chilli flakes

2 tablespoons small basil leaves

2 tablespoons fresh flat-leaf parsley leaves

2 small eggs

50g (1½ ounces) baby spinach leaves

2 thick slices multigrain sourdough bread (140g)

½ clove garlic

1 medium tomato (150g), sliced thickly

½ medium avocado (125g), halved lengthways

2 teaspoons linseeds

1 To make herb salad, toss oil, juice, chilli, basil and parsley in a small bowl; season to taste with pepper.

2 Meanwhile, half fill a large shallow frying pan with water; bring to the boil. Break 1 egg into a cup, then slide into pan; repeat with remaining egg. When both eggs are in pan, return water to the boil. Cover pan, turn off heat; stand for 3 minutes or until a light film of egg white sets over yolks. Using a slotted spoon remove eggs, one at a time, from pan; drain on kitchen paper, cover to keep warm.

3 Place spinach in a heatproof bowl; cover with boiling water, drain immediately. Cool slightly then squeeze out excess liquid.

4 Toast bread, rub warm toast with garlic. Serve toast topped with spinach, tomato, avocado, egg and herb salad; sprinkle with linseeds, season with pepper. Serve immediately.

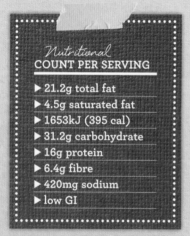

Nutritional
COUNT PER SERVING

▶ 21.2g total fat

▶ 4.5g saturated fat

▶ 1653kJ (395 cal)

▶ 31.2g carbohydrate

▶ 16g protein

▶ 6.4g fibre

▶ 420mg sodium

▶ low GI

berry semolina porridge (recipe opposite)

berry semolina porridge

1 cup (250ml) skim milk

½ cup (125ml) water

1 teaspoon vanilla extract

pinch ground cinnamon

⅓ cup (55g) semolina

1 cup (150g) frozen mixed berries, thawed

¼ cup (70g) low-fat greek yoghurt

2 tablespoons chopped raw pistachios

2 teaspoons honey

1 Combine milk, the water, extract and cinnamon in a medium saucepan. Bring to the boil. Gradually add semolina. Whisk over medium heat for 2 minutes or until thick. Remove from heat; stir in ⅔ cup berries.
2 Divide porridge into serving bowls. Top with yoghurt, nuts, honey and remaining berries.

Use your favourite nuts in this recipe to add crunch and fibre.

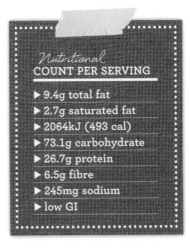

Nutritional COUNT PER SERVING

▶ 9.4g total fat
▶ 2.7g saturated fat
▶ 2064kJ (493 cal)
▶ 73.1g carbohydrate
▶ 26.7g protein
▶ 6.5g fibre
▶ 245mg sodium
▶ low GI

pea fritters with avocado goat's cheese

½ cup (75g) wholemeal self-raising flour

1 teaspoon finely grated lemon rind

1 small egg

½ cup (125ml) skim milk

1 cup (120g) frozen peas, thawed

1 teaspoon rice bran oil

1 small avocado (200g)

30g (1 ounces) fresh goat's cheese, crumbled

2 tablespoons chopped fresh mint leaves

30g (1 ounce) rocket leaves (arugula)

80g (2½ ounces) chopped cherry tomatoes, quartered

2 lemon wedges

1 Combine sifted flour and rind in a medium bowl. Add egg and milk, whisk to combine. Fold through peas. Season with pepper.
2 Heat oil in a large, non-stick frying pan over medium heat; cook ⅓-cups of batter, in batches, for 3 minutes each side or until browned lightly and cooked through. Cover to keep warm.
3 Meanwhile, mash avocado in a small bowl with a fork. Stir through cheese and mint. Serve fritters with avocado mash, rocket, tomato and wedges.

Thaw peas by running under boiling water.
The mixture is quite loose, it will spread once in the pan.

(photograph page 30)

pea fritters with avocado goat's cheese (recipe page 29)

pearl barley and cherry breakfast bowl (recipe page 32)

pearl barley and cherry breakfast bowl

PREP + COOK TIME 50 MINUTES • SERVES 2

½ cup (100g) pearl barley

1½ cups (375ml) water

1 cup (280g) sheep's milk yoghurt

1½ cups (185g) frozen pitted cherries, thawed

2 tablespoons fresh passionfruit pulp

30g (1 ounce) fresh honeycomb, sliced

1 tablespoon chopped fresh mint leaves

2 tablespoons coarsely chopped natural almonds

1 tablespoon sunflower seeds

1 Combine barley and the water in a small saucepan over high heat, bring to the boil; reduce heat to low, cover, simmer for 35 minutes or until tender. Drain; rinse under cold water until cool.

2 Combine barley, yoghurt and ⅔ cup of the cherries in a medium bowl. Divide into serving bowls. Top with remaining cherries, passionfruit, honeycomb, mint, nuts and sunflower seeds.

(photograph page 31)

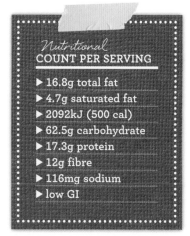

Nutritional
COUNT PER SERVING

▸ 16.8g total fat

▸ 4.7g saturated fat

▸ 2092kJ (500 cal)

▸ 62.5g carbohydrate

▸ 17.3g protein

▸ 12g fibre

▸ 116mg sodium

▸ low GI

baked pina colada granola

PREP + COOK TIME 40 MINUTES • SERVES 2

1 herbal lemon tea bag

¼ cup (60ml) boiling water

1½ cups (135g) rolled oats

2 tablespoons chopped pecans

2 tablespoons sunflower seeds

¼ cup (10g) coconut flakes

¼ cup (40g) chopped dried pineapple

1 cup (250ml) skim milk

1 Preheat oven to 160°C/325°F. Line a large oven tray with baking paper.

2 Combine tea bag and the boiling water in a small heatproof bowl. Stand for 5 minutes. Discard tea bag.

3 Combine oats, nuts and sunflower seeds on tray. Drizzle with tea, stir to coat. Bake for 10 minutes. Stir and bake for a further 10 minutes. Add coconut; bake for 3 minutes or until golden.

4 Stir through pineapple. Cool muesli on tray. Divide into serving bowls. Pour over milk.

Recipe can be doubled and stored in an airtight container; it will last for months if stored correctly.

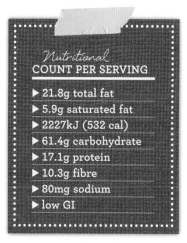

Nutritional
COUNT PER SERVING

▸ 21.8g total fat

▸ 5.9g saturated fat

▸ 2227kJ (532 cal)

▸ 61.4g carbohydrate

▸ 17.1g protein

▸ 10.3g fibre

▸ 80mg sodium

▸ low GI

baked pina colada granola
(recipe opposite)

This recipe serves 4; if serving 2, you can freeze the extra pancakes for up to 3 months. All topping recipes (pages 36-37) serve 2; double if serving 4.

buckwheat pancakes

PREP + COOK TIME 25 MINUTES • **SERVES** 4

1 small egg

1 egg white

2¼ cups (560ml) buttermilk

¾ cup (110g) buckwheat flour

1 cup (150g) wholemeal self-raising flour

2 tablespoons wheat germ

1 Whisk egg, egg white and buttermilk in a large jug. Sift dry ingredients into a large bowl; whisk egg mixture gradually into flour mixture until batter is smooth.

2 Heat an oiled heavy-based medium frying pan over medium heat. Pour ⅓ cup of the batter into pan; cook, uncovered, until bubbles appear on the surface of the pancake. Turn pancake; cook until browned. Remove from pan; cover to keep warm. Repeat with remaining batter to make a total of 8 pancakes.

3 Serve pancakes with selected toppings (see recipes pages 36-37).

Nutritional
COUNT PER SERVING

▶ 5g total fat

▶ 2.5g saturated fat

▶ 1419kJ (339 cal)

▶ 55.2g carbohydrate

▶ 14g protein

▶ 4.9g fibre

▶ 365mg sodium

▶ medium GI

PANCAKE TOPPINGS

You will need 4 pancakes for this recipe.

pancakes with cherry and vanilla compote

PREP + COOK TIME 10 MINUTES • SERVES 2

Make buckwheat pancakes on page 35. Place 2 teaspoons stevia, 1 teaspoon vanilla extract, 2 tablespoons cold water and 100g (3 ounces) pitted cherries in a small saucepan over high heat. Bring to the boil; boil for 5 minutes or until syrup is thickened and cherries are heated through. Cool slightly. Serve over pancakes.

▶ nutritional count per serving 5.5g total fat (2.5g saturated fat); 1550kJ (370 cal); 62g carbohydrate; 14.4g protein; 5.6g fibre; 424mg sodium; medium GI

pancakes with grilled banana and coconut yoghurt

PREP + COOK TIME 10 MINUTES • SERVES 2

Make buckwheat pancakes on page 35. Halve 1 small banana lengthways. Heat an oiled grill plate over medium-high heat; cook banana for 2 minutes each side or until browned and heated through. Combine ¾ teaspoon desiccated coconut with ¼ cup (70g) no-fat greek-style yoghurt. Serve pancakes with banana; accompany with yoghurt topped with an extra ¼ teaspoon desiccated coconut.

▶ nutritional count per serving 5.9g total fat (2.9g saturated fat); 1626kJ (388 cal); 63g carbohydrate; 16.3g protein; 5.6g fibre; 400mg sodium; medium GI

pancakes with toasted maple walnuts

PREP + COOK TIME 15 MINUTES • SERVES 2

Make buckwheat pancakes on page 35. Preheat oven to 180°C/350°F. Line an oven tray with baking paper. Place ⅓ cup (35g) walnuts on tray; drizzle with 1½ teaspoons maple syrup. Bake for 8 minutes, turning halfway through cooking time, or until golden. Set aside to cool, then crumble walnuts. Serve pancakes drizzled with an extra 2 teaspoons maple syrup and walnuts.

▶ nutritional count per serving 17.5g total fat (3.2g saturated fat); 2044kJ (488 cal); 63g carbohydrate; 16.5g protein; 6g fibre; 367mg sodium; medium GI

pancakes with raspberry, honey and mint compote

PREP + COOK TIME 10 MINUTES • SERVES 2

Make buckwheat pancakes on page 35. Place 1½ teaspoons honey, 2 tablespoons cold water and ¾ cup (115g) frozen raspberries in a small saucepan over high heat. Bring to the boil; boil for 5 minutes or until syrup is thickened and raspberries are heated through. Cool slightly, then stir through 2 teaspoons finely shredded mint leaves. Serve over pancakes with extra mint leaves, if you like.

▶ nutritional count per serving 5.5g total fat (2.5g saturated fat); 1620kJ (387 cal); 63g carbohydrate; 14.7g protein; 8.4g fibre; 366mg sodium; medium GI

lunch

rocket, chicken and date salad

PREP + COOK TIME 40 MINUTES (+ COOLING) • SERVES 2

300g (9½ ounces) chicken breast fillet, trimmed

3 cups (750ml) water

1 large orange (300g)

1½ tablespoons lemon juice

3 teaspoons fresh lemon thyme

2 teaspoons extra virgin olive oil

½ medium pomegranate (160g)

70g (2½ ounces) baby rocket leaves (arugula)

4 fresh dates (80g), seeded, quartered lengthways

12 dry roasted natural almonds (15g), chopped coarsely

1 Place chicken and the water in a small saucepan over high heat; bring to the boil. Reduce heat to low; simmer, uncovered, for 10 minutes. Remove from heat; cool for 20 minutes.

2 Meanwhile, using a zester, zest rind from half the orange in long thin strips. Peel orange, cut orange into segments, reserving 1½ tablespoons of juice.

3 To make dressing, combine juices, rind, thyme and oil in a small jug. Season with pepper.

4 Remove seeds from pomegranate; reserve.

5 Remove chicken from poaching liquid; shred chicken coarsely.

6 Arrange rocket on a large serving plate. Drizzle with a little dressing. Top with chicken, orange segments, dates, pomegranate seeds and nuts. Drizzle with remaining dressing.

If you don't have a zester, use a peeler to cut strips of orange rind, then cut the rind into thin strips. The chicken can be cooked a day ahead; cover, refrigerate.

grilled chicken with warm cos lettuce salad

3 slices multigrain bread (100g), cut into 3cm (1¼-inch) cubes

rice bran oil spray

4 small leeks (800g), trimmed, halved lengthways

300g (9½ ounces) chicken breast fillet, trimmed

1 baby cos (romaine) lettuce (185g), trimmed, quartered lengthways

2 teaspoons finely grated lemon rind

1 tablespoon lemon juice

¼ cup coarsely chopped fresh basil leaves

¼ cup coarsely chopped fresh flat-leaf parsley

10g (½ ounce) shaved parmesan cheese

BUTTERMILK DRESSING

¼ cup (60ml) buttermilk

3 teaspoons lemon juice

2 teaspoons chopped fresh tarragon

1 tablespoon chopped fresh chives

½ clove garlic, crushed

1 Preheat oven 200°C/400°F.

2 Place bread on a large oven tray in a single layer, spray with oil; bake for 10 minutes or until golden.

3 Cook leek in a medium pan of boiling water for 4 minutes or until just tender; drain.

4 Heat a lightly oiled grill plate (or grill or barbecue) over high heat; cook chicken for 3 minutes each side or until golden brown. Place chicken on an oven tray; cover with foil. Transfer to oven; bake for 15 minutes or until just cooked through. Rest for 10 minutes, then slice thickly.

5 Meanwhile, spray leeks and lettuce with oil; cook leeks on the grill plate for 3 minutes or until browned and the lettuce for 1 minute or until browned lightly, turning halfway through cooking time.

6 Make buttermilk dressing.

7 Combine chicken in a bowl with rind, juice, basil and parsley.

8 To serve, top lettuce wedges with leeks and chicken mixture; sprinkle with croûtons and parmesan and drizzle with buttermilk dressing. Sprinkle with extra basil and parsley leaves, if you like.

BUTTERMILK DRESSING Combine ingredients in a small jug; season with pepper to taste.

You can substitute leeks with green onions (scallions) or asparagus.

Nutritional
COUNT PER SERVING
▶ 10.2g total fat
▶ 3g saturated fat
▶ 1787kJ (427 cal)
▶ 30.7g carbohydrate
▶ 46.6g protein
▶ 11.9g fibre
▶ 442mg sodium
▶ low GI

lime and coriander beef salad

PREP + COOK TIME 35 MINUTES • **SERVES** 2

80g (2½ ounces) udon noodles

200g (6½ ounces) beef rump steak, trimmed

1 cup loosely packed fresh coriander leaves (cilantro)

1 tablespoon finely grated lime rind

1 lebanese cucumber (130g), cut into ribbons

2 medium tomatoes (300g), chopped coarsely

⅓ cup loosely packed fresh mint leaves

3 green onions (scallions), sliced thinly

100g (3 ounces) snow peas, sliced thinly

50g (1½ ounce) snow pea sprouts

¼ cup (35g) coarsely chopped unsalted roasted cashews

LIME DRESSING

2 tablespoons lime juice

1 teaspoon fish sauce

2 teaspoons finely chopped palm sugar

1 fresh long red chilli, chopped finely

1 Place noodles in a medium heatproof bowl, cover with boiling water; stand for 5 minutes or until just tender, drain. Refresh under cold water; drain.

2 Meanwhile, make dressing.

3 Cook beef on a heated oiled grill plate (or grill or barbecue) for 1 minute each side or until cooked as desired. Cover, rest for 5 minutes.

4 Meanwhile, finely chop half the coriander. Combine chopped coriander and rind on a plate. Coat beef in coriander mixture; slice beef thinly.

5 Add remaining coriander, cucumber, tomato, mint, onion, snow peas, sprouts, dressing and beef to noodles; toss gently to combine. Sprinkle with nuts to serve.

LIME DRESSING Combine ingredients in a screw-top jar; shake to combine.

Use a vegetable peeler to cut cucumber into ribbons.

pumpkin, ricotta and rocket quesadillas

PREP + COOK TIME 1¼ HOURS • SERVES 2

500g (1 pound) butternut pumpkin, peeled, chopped into 4cm (1½-inch) pieces

rice bran oil spray

2 teaspoons each ground cumin and coriander

2 teaspoons coarsely chopped fresh oregano

4 white corn tortillas

50g (1½ ounces) baby rocket leaves (arugula)

⅓ cup (80g) low-fat ricotta

ROASTED CAPSICUM SALSA

1 small red capsicum (bell pepper) (150g), quartered, seeded

1 green onion (scallion), sliced thinly

2 teaspoons coarsely chopped fresh oregano

¼ teaspoon smoked paprika

1 teaspoon balsamic vinegar

1 Preheat oven 200°C/400°F. Line a large baking tray with baking paper.

2 Place pumpkin on baking tray, spray with oil then sprinkle with cumin and coriander; cover with foil. Bake for 45 minutes or until tender. Cool slightly, mash with a fork. Stir in oregano; cool.

3 Meanwhile make roasted capsicum salsa.

4 Spread half the pumpkin mixture over 1 tortilla; top with half the rocket. Spread another tortilla with half the ricotta. Sandwich tortillas and spray both sides with oil spray.

5 Heat a medium non-stick frying pan over medium heat; cook tortillas for 2 minutes each side or until browned and heated through. Repeat with remaining ingredients.

6 Cut quesadillas into wedges; serve with salsa.

ROASTED CAPSICUM SALSA Preheat grill (broiler) to high. Place capsicum, skin-side up, on a large oven tray. Grill for 10 minutes or until skin is blackened. Cover tray with foil. Stand for 10 minutes to cool. Peel and discard skin; roughly chop capsicum. Combine capsicum in a small bowl with remaining ingredients. Season with black pepper to taste.

You can use 120g (4 ounces) drained char-grilled capsicum, if you like.

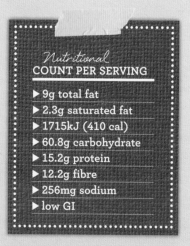

Nutritional
COUNT PER SERVING

▶ 9g total fat
▶ 2.3g saturated fat
▶ 1715kJ (410 cal)
▶ 60.8g carbohydrate
▶ 15.2g protein
▶ 12.2g fibre
▶ 256mg sodium
▶ low GI

spiced vegetable, chickpea and ricotta salad

PREP + COOK TIME 1 HOUR • SERVES 2

200g (6½ ounces) baby carrots, trimmed

1 small kumara (orange sweet potato) (250g), cut into 2cm (¾-inch) wedges

½ small red onion (50g) cut into wedges

½ medium red capsicum (bell pepper) (175g), sliced thickly

½ x 400g (12½ ounces) canned chickpeas (garbanzo beans), rinsed, drained

1 tablespoon rice bran oil

1 teaspoon each ground cumin and coriander

150g (4 ounce) fresh ricotta cheese

large pinch each dried chilli flakes and oregano

150g (4 ounces) vine-ripened baby cherry truss tomatoes

2 tablespoons roughly chopped walnuts

2 tablespoons fresh flat-leaf parsley leaves, torn

1 Preheat oven to 200°C/400°F. Line an oven tray with baking paper.
2 Place carrot, kumara, onion, capsicum and chickpeas on tray. Drizzle with half the oil and sprinkle with cumin and coriander. Toss gently to combine.
3 Place ricotta on tray alongside vegetables. Drizzle with remaining oil; sprinkle with chilli and oregano. Bake ricotta and vegetables for 40 minutes or until vegetables are tender, adding tomatoes to tray for the last 10 minutes of cooking time.
4 Serve ricotta with vegetables sprinkled with nuts and parsley.

You can use heirloom baby carrots, which would add great colour to this dish.

kumara and onion pizza

PREP + COOK TIME 30 MINUTES • SERVES 2

1 small kumara (orange sweet potato) (250g), unpeeled, sliced thinly

½ small brown onion (40g), cut into thin wedges

1 large wholemeal pitta bread (100g)

2 tablespoons salt-reduced tomato pasta sauce

1½ teaspoons finely chopped fresh rosemary

¼ cup (30g) coarsely grated low-fat vintage cheddar cheese

20g (¾ ounce) baby rocket leaves (arugula)

1 Preheat oven to 220°C/425°F. Line an oven tray with baking paper.

2 Cook kumara and onion on a heated oiled grill plate (or grill or barbecue) until browned both sides and tender.

3 Place bread on oven tray; spread with sauce. Layer with vegetables and sprinkle with rosemary then cheese. Bake for 8 minutes or until base is crisp and cheese has melted. Serve topped with rocket.

Nutritional
COUNT PER SERVING

▶ 5.2g total fat
▶ 2.6g saturated fat
▶ 1198kJ (286 cal)
▶ 44.3g carbohydrate
▶ 12g protein
▶ 6.6g fibre
▶ 420mg sodium
▶ medium GI

broad bean, apple & walnut open sandwich (recipe opposite)

broad bean, apple & walnut open sandwich

PREP + COOK TIME 20 MINUTES • SERVES 2

1 cup (150g) frozen broad beans, thawed

1 teaspoon finely grated lemon rind

1 tablespoon lemon juice

1 tablespoon coarsely chopped fresh dill

1 tablespoon coarsely chopped fresh mint

2 trimmed celery stalks (200g), sliced thinly

½ small red apple (65g), sliced thinly

¼ cup (25g) coarsely chopped walnuts

2 thick slices multigrain sourdough bread (140g), toasted

2 tablespoons cashew nut spread

4 baby cos (romaine) lettuce leaves (20g)

5g (¼ ounce) micro watercress

1 Place broad beans in a large heatproof bowl, cover with boiling water; stand for 3 minutes. Rinse under cold water; drain, then peel.

2 Combine beans, rind, juice, dill, mint, celery, apple and walnuts in a large bowl. Season with pepper to taste.

3 Spread bread slices with half the cashew spread each. Top each with a lettuce leaf and half of the bean mixture.

4 Sprinkle with watercress and top with extra lemon rind, if you like.

Cashew spread can be found in the health food aisle of the supermarket or at health food stores.

creamy egg salad open sandwich

PREP + COOK TIME 15 MINUTES • SERVES 2

3 small eggs, at room temperature

2 tablespoons low-fat greek yoghurt

1 tablespoon low-fat mayonnaise

2 teaspoons dijon mustard

2 teaspoons rice bran oil

2 teaspoons baby capers, rinsed, drained, chopped

1 trimmed stalk celery (100g), chopped finely

1 small beetroot (beet) (100g), peeled, grated coarsely

2 red radishes (70g), grated coarsely

2 thin slices rye bread (90g), toasted

1 cup loosely packed watercress leaves (120g)

1 tablespoon finely chopped fresh chives

1 Place eggs in a small saucepan; cover with cold water, cover pan with a lid. Bring water to the boil, then remove lid. Boil for 5 minutes, then remove from heat; drain. When cool enough to handle, shell eggs.

2 Roughly mash eggs in a medium bowl with yoghurt, mayonnaise, mustard, oil, capers and celery.

3 Combine beetroot and radish in a small bowl.

4 Top each bread slice with half the watercress, beetroot and radish mixture, then egg mixture. Sprinkle with chives; season with pepper to taste.

You can make the egg mixture a day ahead. Store in an airtight container in the fridge and assemble sandwiches just before serving.

(photograph page 50)

creamy egg salad open sandwich (recipe page 49)

Nutritional
COUNT PER SERVING

▶ 15.5g total fat
▶ 4.3g saturated fat
▶ 1511kJ (361 cal)
▶ 33.9g carbohydrate
▶ 18.5g protein
▶ 6.2g fibre
▶ 433mg sodium
▶ low GI

roasted brussels sprouts & lentil salad (recipe page 52)

roasted brussels sprouts & lentil salad

¾ cup (150g) dried french-style green lentils

1½ cups (375ml) water

8 brussels sprouts, trimmed, halved

olive-oil spray

2 tablespoons slivered almonds, toasted

¼ cup fresh mint leaves

2 tablespoons low-fat balsamic vinaigrette

2 tablespoons shaved parmesan

1 Place lentils and the water in a small saucepan, bring to the boil over high heat. Reduce heat to low; simmer, covered, for 45 minutes or until lentils are tender. Drain.

2 Preheat oven to 200°C/400°F.

3 Cook sprouts in a small saucepan of boiling water, uncovered, for 3 minutes; drain. Line an oven tray with baking paper. Spread sprouts on tray; spray with oil. Transfer to oven; roast for 20 minutes or until golden.

4 Place lentils, sprouts, nuts, mint, vinaigrette and parmesan in a bowl; season with pepper to taste. Toss to combine.

This is a great side for grilled chicken or fish. If brussels sprouts aren't available you can use chopped cabbage.

(photograph page 51)

tomato & white bean puree salad

80g (2½ ounce) ciabatta bread, torn

200g (12 ½ ounces) canned cannellini beans, rinsed, drained

1 garlic clove, crushed

2 teaspoons lemon juice

2 teaspoons rice bran oil

200g (6 ½ ounces) medley tomatoes, sliced

3 teaspoons red wine vinegar

2 tablespoons small fresh basil leaves

1 Preheat grill (broiler) to high. Place bread on an oven tray; grill for 1 minute or until browned lightly.

2 Blend or process beans, garlic, juice and oil until mixture is smooth. Season with pepper to taste.

3 Combine tomato, vinegar and two-thirds of the basil in a small bowl; toss gently to combine. Serve bean mixture topped with tomato salad and bread; sprinkle with remaining basil.

Depending on the brand of beans used, you may need to add 1 tablespoon water to reach the desired consistency.

tomato & white bean purée salad (recipe opposite)

ginger and chilli chicken rice paper rolls

50g (1½ ounces) rice vermicelli noodles

2 tablespoons finely grated ginger

1 teaspoon peanut oil

2 teaspoons lime juice

2 teaspoons chinese cooking wine

2 skinless cooked chicken breast fillets (400g), sliced thickly

6 x 22cm (9-inch) rice paper rounds

12 fresh coriander (cilantro) sprigs

1 small carrot (70g), grated coarsely

2 green onions (scallions), halved lengthways, cut into matchsticks

½ small red capsicum (bell pepper) (150g), cut into matchsticks

½ lebanese cucumber (65g), cut into matchsticks

½ long red chilli, seeded, sliced thinly

⅓ cup bean sprouts (25g)

1 Place vermicelli in a large heatproof bowl; cover with boiling water, separate noodles with a fork. Stand until tender; drain.

2 Place ginger in a fine sieve over a medium bowl; press down firmly on ginger to remove juice; discard pulp. Add oil, lime juice and cooking wine to ginger juice. Gently toss chicken and noodles through the ginger mixture.

3 Dip one rice paper round into a bowl of warm water until soft. Lift sheet from water; place on a clean tea towel. Place two coriander sprigs on the rice paper, top with one-sixth of the noodle mixture, carrot, onion, capsicum, cucumber, chilli and sprouts. Fold rice sheet over filling, then fold in both sides. Continue rolling to enclose filling, repeat with remaining ingredients to make a total of 6 rolls. Serve with a wedge of lime, if you like.

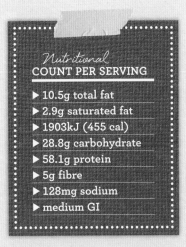

Nutritional
COUNT PER SERVING

▶ 10.5g total fat
▶ 2.9g saturated fat
▶ 1903kJ (455 cal)
▶ 28.8g carbohydrate
▶ 58.1g protein
▶ 5g fibre
▶ 128mg sodium
▶ medium GI

thai prawn burger

1 clove garlic

2 coriander roots (cilantro), with 1cm (½-inch) stem attached

2 teaspoons coarsely chopped fresh ginger

2 kaffir lime leaves, shredded

2 fresh long red chillies, sliced thinly

8 uncooked, peeled small king prawns (shrimp) (100g), chopped finely

1 small potato (120g), coarsely grated

1 tablespoon rice bran oil

3 teaspoons lime juice

2 small wholemeal bread rolls (85g), split in half crossways

4 medium butter lettuce leaves

½ small red onion (40g), sliced thinly

20g (¾ ounce) bean sprouts

½ lebanese cucumber (65g), cut into ribbons

⅓ cup fresh coriander leaves (cilantro)

1 Combine garlic, coriander root and stems, ginger, kaffir lime leaves and half the chilli in a mortar and pestle, pound until mixture forms a thick paste. Divide paste in half.

2 Combine half of the paste with prawns and potato in a small bowl; using wet hands form mixture into two patties. Cover, refrigerate 2 hours or overnight.

3 Add half the oil and 2 teaspoons of juice to the remaining paste in a small bowl. Cover, refrigerate until required.

4 Heat remaining oil in a small non-stick frying pan over low heat; cook patties for 3 minutes each side or until cooked through. Transfer to a plate; drizzle patties with remaining juice.

5 Place bread rolls, cut-side down, in same pan for 1 minute or until warm.

6 Toss lettuce, onion, sprouts, cucumber, coriander leaves and remaining chilli through reserved paste. Sandwich salad mixture and patties between rolls.

Nutritional
COUNT PER SERVING

▶ 11.1g total fat
▶ 1.7g saturated fat
▶ 1271kJ (304 cal)
▶ 29.5g carbohydrate
▶ 17.7g protein
▶ 6.7g fibre
▶ 428mg sodium
▶ high GI

Test Kitchen
NOTES

The remaining bread can
be frozen or processed
into breadcrumbs and
frozen to make foods such
as fishcakes, schnitzels
and potato bake toppings.
Leave the chilli seeds in
if you prefer more heat.

mixed mushroom trencher with herb salad

PREP + COOK TIME 30 MINUTES • SERVES 2

In medieval times a 'trencher' was a cut from a round of stale bread and used as a 'plate'.

2 teaspoons rice bran oil

150g (4½ ounces) swiss brown mushrooms, sliced thickly

3 portobello mushrooms (150g), sliced thickly

100g (3 ounces) enoki mushrooms, base trimmed

2 teaspoons fresh lemon thyme leaves

1 small fresh thai red chilli (serrano), seeded, chopped finely

1 clove garlic, crushed

1 teaspoon lemon juice

1 wholemeal sourdough loaf (675g)

1 clove garlic, halved crossways, extra

HERB SALAD

½ teaspoon cumin seeds

1 teaspoon coarsely chopped sunflower seeds

1 teaspoon black chia seeds

2 teaspoons rice bran oil

2 teaspoons lemon juice

½ small red onion (50g), sliced thinly

⅓ cup each fresh flat-leaf parsley and mint leaves

1 tablespoon each fresh dill sprigs and small tarragon leaves

1 Preheat grill (broiler) to high.

2 Make herb salad.

3 Heat oil in a large non-stick frying pan over high heat; cook mushrooms, thyme and chilli, stirring occasionally, for 4 minutes or until browned lightly. Add garlic; cook for 1 minute or until fragrant. Remove from heat, stir through juice. Season with pepper to taste. Cover to keep warm.

4 Cut bread 2cm (¾-inch) from the base lengthways, you will need 175g (5½ ounces) of bread (save the upper portion for another use, see notes). Place bread base on a large oven tray; grill for 1 minute or until toasted lightly. Rub warm bread with extra garlic clove.

5 Top bread with mushrooms and any juices. Top with salad. Cut in half to serve.

HERB SALAD Heat a large non-stick frying pan over medium heat; cook cumin, sunflower and chia seeds, stirring, for 2 minutes or until seeds are toasted, transfer to a small bowl. Add remaining ingredients; toss to combine.

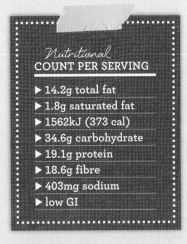

Nutritional
COUNT PER SERVING

▸ 14.2g total fat
▸ 1.8g saturated fat
▸ 1562kJ (373 cal)
▸ 34.6g carbohydrate
▸ 19.1g protein
▸ 18.6g fibre
▸ 403mg sodium
▸ low GI

noodle salad with ginger-rubbed beef

PREP + COOK TIME 25 MINUTES • SERVES 2

100g (3 ounces) soba noodles

200g (6½ ounces) rump steak, trimmed

2 teaspoons peanut oil

1 tablespoon finely grated fresh ginger

1 small zucchini (180g), cut into ribbons

1 small carrot (70g), cut into ribbons

60g (2 ounces) drained canned water chestnuts, sliced thinly

1 cup (80g) bean sprouts

½ cup fresh thai basil leaves

½ cup fresh coriander (cilantro) leaves

2 tablespoons lime juice

½ teaspoon sesame oil

1 clove garlic, crushed

3 teaspoons honey

1 teaspoon sodium-reduced soy sauce

2 tablespoons unsalted roasted peanuts, chopped coarsely

1 Cook noodles in a medium saucepan of boiling water, uncovered, for 4 minutes. Drain, rinse under cold water; drain well.

2 Rub steak with combined peanut oil and half the ginger. Season with pepper. Cook steak in a small heated non-stick frying pan for 2 minutes each side for medium or until cooked as desired. Stand covered for 5 minutes, then slice thinly.

3 Combine noodles, zucchini, carrot, chestnuts, sprouts, basil and coriander in a large bowl.

4 Combine remaining ginger, juice, sesame oil, garlic, honey and sauce in a screw-top jar; shake well. Pour over salad, toss gently to combine. Divide salad into serving bowls; top with steak, sprinkle with nuts.

You could also try this with ginger-rubbed chicken breast or firm tofu. Use a vegetable peeler or mandoline to cut vegetables into ribbons.

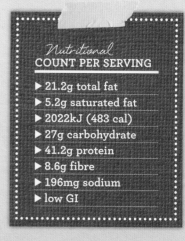

Nutritional
COUNT PER SERVING

▶ 21.2g total fat
▶ 5.2g saturated fat
▶ 2022kJ (483 cal)
▶ 27g carbohydrate
▶ 41.2g protein
▶ 8.6g fibre
▶ 196mg sodium
▶ low GI

chai roasted pumpkin soup with honey walnuts

PREP + COOK TIME 50 MINUTES • SERVES 2

1kg (2 pounds) pumpkin, peeled, chopped coarsely

½ teaspoon ground cardamom

¼ teaspoon ground cinnamon

½ teaspoon cracked black pepper

olive-oil spray

¼ cup (25g) walnuts

1 teaspoon honey

2 teaspoons rice bran oil

1 small brown onion (80g), chopped coarsely

2 cloves garlic, sliced

¾ cup (180ml) salt-reduced vegetable stock

1¾ cups (430ml) water

⅓ cup (95g) low-fat greek yoghurt

2 tablespoons roughly chopped fresh coriander leaves (cilantro)

1 Preheat oven to 200°C/400°F. Line a large oven tray with baking paper.

2 Place pumpkin on tray, in a single layer; sprinkle with cardamom, cinnamon and pepper, spray with oil. Roast for 25 minutes or until tender.

3 Meanwhile, line a small oven tray with baking paper. Place nuts on tray, drizzle with honey. Roast for 5 minutes or until golden. Cool.

4 Heat rice bran oil in a large saucepan over medium heat. Cook onion and garlic, stirring, for 5 minutes or until softened. Add pumpkin, stock and the water to the pan; bring to the boil. Remove from heat; cool for 10 minutes.

5 Blend or process pumpkin mixture until smooth. Return pan to heat, stir until hot. To serve, drizzle soup with yoghurt; sprinkle with nuts and coriander.

You can freeze the soup in airtight containers.

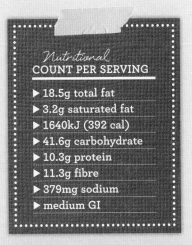

Nutritional
COUNT PER SERVING

▶ 18.5g total fat

▶ 3.2g saturated fat

▶ 1640kJ (392 cal)

▶ 41.6g carbohydrate

▶ 10.3g protein

▶ 11.3g fibre

▶ 379mg sodium

▶ medium GI

4 Ways with LENTILS

asparagus & fennel salad
PREP + COOK TIME 1 HOUR • SERVES 2

Bring ½ cup (100g) dried brown lentils to the boil;
simmer, covered, for 45 minutes or until tender,
drain. Spray 6 asparagus spears and half a finely
sliced fennel bulb with oil; cook on a heated grill
plate for 3 minutes or until brown and tender.
Combine vegetables in a large bowl with lentils,
½ cup cooked brown rice, ½ cup fresh flat-leaf
parsley leaves, ¼ cup toasted pepitas, 2 tablespoons
finely chopped fresh chives and ¼ cup sliced green
olives. Drizzle with 2 tablespoons lemon juice and
2 teaspoons rice bran oil. Season with pepper.

▶ **nutritional count per serving** 21g total fat
(3.1g saturated fat); 2023kJ (483 cal); 43.8g carbohydrate;
23.2g protein; 14.7g fibre; 267mg sodium; low GI

beetroot & hazelnut salad
PREP + COOK TIME 1½ HOURS • SERVES 2

Bring ⅔ cup (130g) dried brown lentils to the boil;
simmer, covered, for 45 minutes or until tender,
drain. Preheat oven to 200°C/400°F. Place 1 bunch
trimmed and washed baby beetroot (beet) on a large
oven tray; cover with foil. Roast for 30 minutes. Add
1 bunch trimmed, peeled baby carrots, spray with
olive oil; roast, uncovered, for a further 30 minutes
or until tender. Peel and halve beetroot; combine on
a serving platter with carrots, lentils, 2 cups baby
rocket (arugula), 2 sliced green onions (scallions)
and ¼ cup roasted chopped hazelnuts. Drizzle with
2 tablespoons lemon juice and toss gently to combine.

▶ **nutritional count per serving** 13.8g total fat
(0.8g saturated fat); 1884kJ (450 cal); 46.5g carbohydrate;
22.1g protein; 24.3g fibre; 212mg sodium; low GI

lentil & herb tabbouleh
PREP + COOK TIME 1 HOUR • SERVES 2

Bring ⅓ cup (65g) dried brown lentils to the boil; simmer, covered, for 45 minutes or until tender, drain. Combine 1 finely chopped small yellow capsicum (bell pepper), 2 finely chopped medium tomatoes, ⅔ cup finely chopped fresh flat-leaf parsley, ¼ cup finely chopped fresh mint leaves, 1 teaspoon finely grated lemon rind, 2 tablespoons lemon juice, ¼ teaspoon dried chilli flakes, 1 tablespoon rice bran oil and lentils in a large bowl; toss gently to combine. Accompany each serving with one slice of sourdough bread (25g).

▶ nutritional count per serving 10.7g total fat (1.6g saturated fat); 1226kJ (293 cal); 29.3g carbohydrate; 14.4g protein; 10.8g fibre; 151mg sodium; low GI

spiced lentil & egg salad
PREP + COOK TIME 1 HOUR • SERVES 2

Bring ⅔ cup (130g) dried brown lentils to the boil; simmer, covered, for 45 minutes or until tender, drain. Cook 2 eggs in boiling water for 6 minutes; cool, shell, then halve eggs. Combine lentils in a bowl with 200g (6½ ounces) blanched sliced green beans and 1 teaspoon curry powder. Top lentil mixture with eggs and 2 tablespoons roughly chopped parsley leaves. Serve with ¼ cup light tzatziki and 1 tablespoon mango chutney.

▶ nutritional count per serving 7.3g total fat (1.8g saturated fat); 1121kJ (289 cal); 29.1g carbohydrate; 22.9g protein; 10g fibre; 340mg sodium; low GI

dinner

barbecued squid with lemon cracked wheat risotto

PREP + COOK TIME 45 MINUTES • SERVES 2

200g (6½ ounces) squid hoods, halved

1 clove garlic, crushed

2 teaspoons chopped fresh oregano

1 teaspoon finely grated lemon rind

1 tablespoon olive oil

1 small brown onion (80g), chopped finely

2 cloves garlic, crushed, extra

2 teaspoons fresh lemon thyme leaves

½ cup (80g) coarse cracked wheat

2 cups (500ml) water

1 cup (120g) frozen peas

1 tablespoon lemon juice

2 teaspoons fresh oregano leaves, extra

1 Score the inside of the squid with a small sharp knife; cut into 4cm (1½-inch) strips. Combine in a bowl with garlic, chopped oregano, rind and 2 teaspoons of oil.

2 Heat remaining oil in a medium non-stick frying pan over medium heat; cook onion, extra garlic and thyme, stirring, for 5 minutes or until softened.

3 Add cracked wheat and the water; cook, stirring occasionally, for 15 minutes or until cracked wheat is tender. Add peas and juice, stir for 2 minutes or until heated through.

4 Meanwhile, cook squid on a heated grill plate (or grill or barbecue) for 2 minutes, turning halfway through cooking time, or until just cooked through.

5 Slice squid. Serve cracked wheat with squid; sprinkle with extra oregano.

You could also try this with thin strips of chicken or pork. Cracked wheat can be bought from health food stores.

korean beef lettuce cups with pickled vegetables

1 fresh long red chilli, chopped coarsely

1 tablespoon coarsely chopped lemon grass

2 cloves garlic, halved

2 teaspoons finely chopped fresh ginger

1 tablespoon water

3 teaspoons reduced-salt soy sauce

150g (4½ ounces) lean beef sirloin steak, trimmed, thinly sliced

½ cup (100g) low-GI brown rice (doongara)

2 teaspoons rice bran oil

6 large butter lettuce leaves (50g)

1 teaspoon sesame oil

¼ cup firmly packed fresh coriander leaves (cilantro)

½ cup (40g) bean sprouts, trimmed

PICKLED CABBAGE

1 fresh long red chilli, chopped finely

1 small carrot (70g), cut into matchsticks

1½ cups (120g) shredded green cabbage

2 teaspoons caster (superfine) sugar

1 tablespoon rice wine vinegar

1 Blend or process chilli, lemon grass, garlic, ginger, the water and half the sauce until smooth. Combine chilli mixture and beef in a small bowl. Cover; refrigerate for 30 minutes.

2 Cook rice in a medium saucepan of boiling water, stirring occasionally, for 25 minutes or until tender; drain well.

3 Meanwhile, make pickled cabbage.

4 Heat rice bran oil in a wok over high heat; cook beef, in batches, for 30 seconds or until browned all over.

5 Spoon rice into lettuce leaves, top with some of the pickled cabbage, then some of the beef. Combine remaining sauce and sesame oil; drizzle over beef. Sprinkle with coriander and sprouts.

PICKLED CABBAGE Combine ingredients in a large bowl. Stand for 30 minutes to soften and develop the flavours.

Freeze beef slightly to make it easier to cut into thin slices. Remove seeds from chilli for a milder heat.

barbecued steak with white bean puree and chimichurri

PREP + COOK TIME 2 HOURS (+ STANDING) • SERVES 2

½ cup dried cannellini beans

4 cloves garlic, peeled

1½ tablespoons lemon juice

¼ cup (60ml) water

150g (4½ ounces) lean beef skirt steak, trimmed

1 teaspoon rice bran oil

1 tablespoon coarsely chopped fresh oregano

2 cups (230g) watercress sprigs

½ small red onion (50g), sliced thinly

CHIMICHURRI

1¼ cups fresh flat-leaf parsley leaves, chopped finely

¼ cup fresh oregano leaves, chopped finely

1 clove garlic, crushed

¼ teaspoon chilli flakes

1 tablespoon red wine vinegar

2 teaspoons dijon mustard

1 teaspoon rice bran oil

1 Place beans in a large bowl; cover with cold water. Stand overnight. Drain.

2 Cook beans and garlic in a large saucepan of boiling water for 1½ hours or until very tender. Drain well.

3 Blend or process beans, garlic, juice and the water until smooth. Season with pepper to taste. Transfer to a small bowl, cover to keep warm.

4 Meanwhile, make chimichurri.

5 Drizzle steaks with oil, sprinkle with oregano. Heat a grill pan (or grill or barbecue) over medium high heat; cook beef for 3 minutes each side for medium or until cooked as desired. Transfer to a plate; cover, stand for 10 minutes.

6 Slice beef; serve with bean puree, chimichurri and combined watercress and onion.

CHIMICHURRI Combine ingredients in a small bowl; mix well. Season with pepper to taste.

You will need 1½ cups cooked beans. You can use 60g (2 ounces) baby rocket leaves (arugula) instead of watercress, if you like.

Nutritional
COUNT PER SERVING

▶ 10.2g total fat
▶ 2.4g saturated fat
▶ 1509kJ (360 cal)
▶ 27g carbohydrate
▶ 32.3g protein
▶ 19.3g fibre
▶ 172mg sodium
▶ low GI

beetroot and lamb flat breads with tahini yoghurt

PREP + COOK TIME 50 MINUTES (+ STANDING) • SERVES 2

¼ cup (40g) wholemeal plain (all-purpose) flour

½ cup (75g) plain (all-purpose) flour

⅓ cup (80ml) water, approximately

2 teaspoons rice bran oil

1 small red onion (100g), sliced thinly

100g (3 ounces) lean minced (ground) lamb

3 cloves garlic, crushed

2 teaspoons ground cumin

¼ teaspoon chilli flakes

100g (3 ounces) canned drained beetroot (beet) wedges

125g (4 ounces) cherry tomatoes, halved

2 tablespoons each fresh mint and coriander (cilantro) leaves

TAHINI YOGHURT

¼ cup (70g) no-fat plain yoghurt

2 teaspoons tahini (sesame seed paste)

1 clove garlic, crushed

2 teaspoons lemon juice

2 teaspoons coarsely chopped fresh coriander (cilantro)

2 teaspoons coarsely chopped fresh mint

½ teaspoon ground cumin

2 teaspoons water

1 Combine sifted flours in a large bowl. Add enough of the water to mix to a soft dough. Turn out onto a lightly floured surface. Knead gently for 1 minute or until smooth. Divide dough into two portions. Cover, stand for 30 minutes.

2 Heat oil in a large non-stick frying pan over medium-low heat; cook onion, stirring, for 5 minutes or until soft. Add mince; cook, stirring, over high heat, for 5 minutes or until browned. Add garlic, cumin and chilli; cook, stirring, for 1 minute or until fragrant. Season with pepper to taste.

3 Preheat oven to 220°C/425°F. Roll one piece of dough between two pieces of baking paper to make a 30cm (12-inch) oval. Discard top sheet of paper. Transfer bottom sheet of baking paper and dough onto a large baking tray. Top with half the lamb mixture, half the beetroot and half the tomato. Repeat with remaining dough, lamb, beetroot and tomato to make two flat breads.

4 Bake for 15 minutes, swapping trays halfway through cooking time, or until bases are browned and crisp.

5 Meanwhile, make tahini yoghurt.

6 Drizzle flat breads with tahini yoghurt; sprinkle with mint and coriander leaves, to serve.

TAHINI YOGHURT Combine ingredients in a small bowl; season with pepper.

Dough can be made ahead; store, covered, in the fridge.

lamb cutlets with smashed potatoes and brussels sprouts salad

PREP + COOK TIME 1 HOUR • SERVES 2

2 medium potatoes (400g)

2 teaspoons rice bran oil

1 tablespoon fennel seeds

1 tablespoon fresh rosemary leaves

6 french-trimmed lamb cutlets (300g)

1 tablespoon honey

1 tablespoon lemon juice

¼ cup (60ml) water

1½ cups shredded cavolo nero (tuscan cabbage) (200g)

12 brussels sprouts (370g), sliced finely

1 tablespoon balsamic vinegar

1 Preheat oven to 220°C/425°F. Line an oven tray with baking paper.

2 Cook potatoes in a small saucepan of boiling water for 10 minutes or until tender; drain. Place potatoes on oven tray; crush with a potato masher. Drizzle with half the oil, sprinkle with half the fennel seeds and half the rosemary. Season with ground black pepper. Bake for 30 minutes or until browned and crisp.

3 Meanwhile, coat lamb in remaining oil; sprinkle with remaining fennel seeds and rosemary. Heat an oiled grill plate (or grill or barbecue) over medium-high heat; cook cutlets for 3 minutes each side or until browned and tender. Transfer to a plate; drizzle with honey and half the juice. Cover; stand for 5 minutes.

4 Heat a large frying pan over high heat, add the water, cavolo nero and sprouts; cook, stirring, for 2 minutes or until vegetables are just tender. Toss through vinegar and the remaining juice.

5 Serve cutlets and potatoes with vegetables.

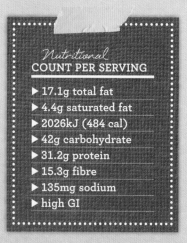

Nutritional
COUNT PER SERVING

▶ 17.1g total fat

▶ 4.4g saturated fat

▶ 2026kJ (484 cal)

▶ 42g carbohydrate

▶ 31.2g protein

▶ 15.3g fibre

▶ 135mg sodium

▶ high GI

Test Kitchen
NOTES

Use a mandoline or a
V-slicer to thinly slice
the brussels sprouts. If
brussels sprouts are not
in season, try making the
salad with thinly sliced
broccoli or shredded
cabbage. Silver beet or
kale can be substituted
for cavolo nero.

kaffir lime and red curry fish parcels

PREP + COOK TIME 30 MINUTES (+ REFRIGERATION) • SERVES 2

2 teaspoons red curry paste

4 shredded kaffir lime leaves

2 coriander roots (cilantro) with 1cm (½-inch) of stem, bruised

1 fresh long red chilli, sliced finely

2 x 200g (7 ounces) firm boneless white fish fillets, skin on

1 small kumara (orange sweet potato) (250g), cut into 1cm (½-inch) thick slices

2 teaspoons lime juice

2 tablespoons red quinoa

2 teaspoons light coconut milk

2 tablespoons fresh coriander (cilantro) leaves

1 Combine paste, lime leaves, coriander roots and stems, and half the chilli in a small bowl. Rub fish fillets with mixture; cover, refrigerate for 1 hour or overnight.

2 Preheat oven to 220°C/425°F.

3 Place kumara in a small saucepan, cover with cold water; bring to the boil, simmer, uncovered, for 5 minutes or until just tender, drain.

4 Cut two pieces of foil 50cm x 30cm (19-inches x 12-inches); place on work surface, shiny-side up. Lay two 48cm x 30cm (18-inch x 12-inch) pieces of baking paper over foil.

5 Divide kumara and fish mixture between paper, drizzle with juice. Fold foil over to completely enclose fish and kumara.

6 Place fish parcels on a large baking tray. Bake parcels for 15 minutes or until fish is cooked through. Discard coriander roots and stems.

7 Meanwhile, rinse and drain quinoa well. Place in a small saucepan, cover with water; bring to the boil, boil for 10 minutes or until tender, drain.

8 Serve fish with quinoa; top with coconut milk, remaining chilli and coriander leaves.

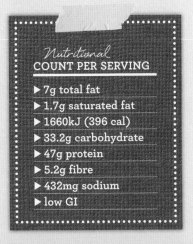

Nutritional
COUNT PER SERVING

▶ 7g total fat
▶ 1.7g saturated fat
▶ 1660kJ (396 cal)
▶ 33.2g carbohydrate
▶ 47g protein
▶ 5.2g fibre
▶ 432mg sodium
▶ low GI

chicken and pumpkin pot pies

PREP + COOK TIME 45 MINUTES • SERVES 2

250g (8 ounces) chicken breast fillet

450g (14½ ounces) butternut pumpkin, chopped coarsely

1 small leek (200g), sliced thinly

1 clove garlic, crushed

¼ teaspoon thyme leaves

¼ cup (60ml) water

1 teaspoon plain (all-purpose) flour

2 sheets fillo pastry

1 egg white, beaten lightly

1 teaspoon coarsely chopped pepitas

30g (1 ounce) firmly packed small beetroot leaves

1 teaspoon lemon juice

1 Place chicken in a medium saucepan; cover with cold water. Bring to the boil; reduce heat, simmer, uncovered, for 10 minutes or until chicken is cooked through. Drain chicken reserving ½ cup of the poaching liquid. Shred chicken.

2 Meanwhile, boil, steam or microwave pumpkin until tender; mash coarsely.

3 Preheat oven to 200°C/400°F.

4 Cook leek, garlic, thyme and the water in a medium saucepan over medium heat, stirring occasionally, for 5 minutes or until leek is tender. Add flour; cook, stirring, for 2 minutes or until slightly thickened. Add chicken, reserved poaching liquid and pumpkin, bring to the boil, stirring, for 2 minutes or until thickened slightly. Season with pepper to taste.

5 Brush pastry sheets with egg white, folding in half three times to make a square. Brush edges of two 1-cup (250ml) heatproof ramekins with egg white. Divide chicken mixture between ramekins, top with pastry squares turning edges of pastry upwards. Brush tops with egg white. Using a small sharp knife, make a hole in the centre of each pie; sprinkle with pepitas. Bake pies for 25 minutes or until pastry is browned lightly.

6 Combine beetroot leaves and juice in a small bowl, season with pepper to taste. Serve hot pies with beetroot leaves.

Filling can be prepared up to two days ahead; store, covered, in the fridge.

pork and sage meatballs with cabbage and pear

PREP + COOK TIME 40 MINUTES (+ REFRIGERATION) • SERVES 2

175g (5½ ounces) lean minced (ground) pork

⅓ cup (25g) fresh multigrain breadcrumbs

1 small egg white

1 teaspoon finely grated lemon rind

½ teaspoon allspice

1 small brown onion (80g), grated coarsely

1 tablespoon chopped fresh sage leaves

2 tablespoons chopped fresh flat-leaf parsley leaves

2 teaspoons rice bran oil

1 small leek (200g), halved, sliced thinly

1 medium pear (230g), sliced thinly

85g (3 ounces) broccolini, trimmed

2 cups (160g) finely shredded red cabbage

½ teaspoon caraway seeds

1 tablespoon small sage leaves

1 tablespoon sultanas

1 Combine pork, breadcrumbs, egg white, rind, allspice, onion, chopped sage and parsley in a medium bowl; mix well. Form mixture into six balls. Place on a tray; cover, refrigerate for 30 minutes to firm.

2 Heat half the oil in a large non-stick frying pan over low heat; cook meatballs, turning, for 8 minutes or until browned and cooked through. Transfer to a clean tray; cover with foil to keep warm.

3 Heat remaining oil in a large saucepan over medium-high heat; cook leek, stirring, for 3 minutes. Add pear and broccolini; cook, turning occasionally, for 3 minutes. Add cabbage, caraway, sage leaves and sultanas; cook, stirring, for 3 minutes or until just tender.

4 Serve vegetables with meatballs.

You could double the meatball recipe to serve 4 or freeze a batch for another meal. Meatballs will freeze for up to 3 months; thaw overnight in the fridge before cooking.

Nutritional
COUNT PER SERVING

▶ 11.8g total fat

▶ 3.1g saturated fat

▶ 1542kJ (368 cal)

▶ 32.8g carbohydrate

▶ 26.8g protein

▶ 13.4g fibre

▶ 196mg sodium

▶ low GI

smokey burghul salad with kingfish

Nutritional
COUNT PER SERVING

- ▶ 13.2 g total fat
- ▶ 2.3g saturated fat
- ▶ 1927kJ (460 cal)
- ▶ 49g carbohydrate
- ▶ 30.1g protein
- ▶ 11.3g fibre
- ▶ 87mg sodium
- ▶ low GI

½ cup (80g) fine burghul

250g (8 ounces) kumara (orange sweet potato), chopped finely

1 small red onion (100g), cut into thin wedges

1 small red capsicum (bell pepper) (150g), chopped coarsely

1 large zucchini (150g), chopped coarsely

2 teaspoons smoked paprika

2 cloves garlic, crushed

1 tablespoon rice bran oil

2 tablespoons white wine vinegar

2 x 100g (3 ounce) kingfish fillets

2 tablespoons coarsely chopped fresh flat-leaf parsley leaves

2 lemon wedges

1 Place burghul in a medium bowl, cover with cold water; stand for 1 hour. Drain.
2 Preheat oven to 200°C/400°F. Line a large oven tray with baking paper.
3 Combine kumara, onion, capsicum, zucchini, paprika, garlic and oil, in a single layer, on tray. Roast for 30 minutes or until browned and tender. Add burghul and vinegar, mix to combine.
4 Meanwhile, cook fish in a large heated oiled frying pan for 2 minutes each side or until browned and cooked through.
5 Serve salad topped with fish, parsley and wedges.

If you can't get burghul you could use couscous instead. Fine burghul can be bought at supermarkets and health food stores.

roasted eggplant with spiced lamb

PREP + COOK TIME 45 MINUTES • SERVES 2

1 large eggplant (500g), halved lengthways

2 teaspoons olive oil

350g (11 ounces) cauliflower, chopped coarsely

150g (4½ ounces) lean minced (ground) lamb

1 teaspoon each ground cumin and coriander

2 tablespoons water

2 teaspoons pomegranate molasses

½ cup (140g) fat-free natural yoghurt

2 teaspoons lemon juice

1 clove garlic, crushed

2 tablespoons currants

½ cup fresh coriander leaves (cilantro)

½ teaspoon sumac

1 Preheat oven to 200°C/400°F. Line a large oven tray with baking paper.

2 Using a sharp knife, score the eggplant flesh diagonally. Drizzle with half the oil. Place flesh-side down on tray. Roast for 10 minutes. Add cauliflower to tray; drizzle with remaining oil. Roast a further 30 minutes or until tender.

3 Meanwhile, heat a medium oiled non-stick frying pan over high heat; cook lamb, spices and the water, stirring, until browned. Add pomegranate molasses. Remove from heat.

4 Combine yoghurt, juice and garlic in a small bowl.

5 Serve eggplant topped with cauliflower, lamb, currants and coriander. Spoon over yoghurt mixture and sprinkle with sumac.

Sumac is a spice made from ground berries and has a lemony flavour. It is available from supermarkets and spice shops.

Nutritional
COUNT PER SERVING

▶ 11.3g total fat

▶ 3.2g saturated fat

▶ 1424kJ (340 cal)

▶ 27g carbohydrate

▶ 26.7g protein

▶ 12.1g fibre

▶ 186mg sodium

▶ low GI

pasta with spinach mushrooms & almonds (recipe opposite)

pasta with spinach, mushrooms & almonds

PREP + COOK TIME 30 MINUTES · SERVES 2

200g (6½ ounces) wholegrain spaghetti

3 teaspoons rice bran oil

300g (10 ounces) swiss brown mushrooms, sliced

300g (10 ounces) portobello mushrooms, sliced

1 shallot (25g), chopped coarsely

1 clove garlic, chopped coarsely

1 tablespoon firmly packed fresh flat-leaf parsley

¼ cup (40g) coarsely chopped unsalted, roasted almonds

100g (3 ounces) baby spinach leaves

¼ cup (20g) flaked pecorino cheese

1 Cook pasta in a large saucepan of boiling water until tender; reserve ½ cup liquid, drain pasta.
2 Meanwhile, heat oil in a large frying pan over high heat; cook mushrooms and shallot, stirring occasionally, for 5 minutes or until mushrooms are lightly golden and shallot is tender. Add garlic and parsley; cook, stirring, for 1 minute or until garlic is fragrant. Season to taste with black pepper.
3 Reduce heat to low; toss warm pasta, nuts and spinach through mushroom mixture. Add enough reserved pasta water to lightly coat the pasta. Serve topped with cheese.

You can use 600g (1¼ ounces) of your favourite variety of mushrooms; button and cap mushrooms will work well. If you don't have a large frying pan, cook the mushrooms in batches to prevent them stewing.

salmon with green papaya & pink grapefruit salad

PREP + COOK TIME 35 MINUTES · SERVES 2

100g (3 ounces) dry egg noodles

1 lebanese cucumber (130g), cut into ribbons

70g (2½ ounces) shredded green papaya

3 shallots (75g), sliced finely

1 small ruby grapefruit (350g), peeled, segmented

1 fresh long red chilli, chopped finely

½ cup loosely packed fresh mint leaves

½ cup loosely packed fresh coriander (cilantro) leaves

½ cup loosely packed fresh thai basil leaves

1 tablespoon shredded kaffir lime leaves

2 tablespoons lime juice

1 teaspoon fish sauce

1 tablespoon brown sugar

2 teaspoons rice bran oil

200g (6½ ounces) skinless salmon fillet, trimmed, halved lengthways

1 Cook noodles according to packet directions. Drain, rinse under cold water.
2 Meanwhile, combine cucumber, papaya, shallot, grapefruit, chilli, herbs and lime leaves in a large bowl. Drizzle with combined juice, sauce and sugar; toss gently to combine.
3 Heat oil in a medium non-stick frying pan over high heat; cook fish for 2 minutes each side or until just cooked through.
4 Serve fish with salad and noodles.

Swap the salmon for tuna steaks if you like. If papaya is unavailable you could use green mango. Remove the seeds from the chilli to reduce the heat.

(photograph page 86)

salmon with green papaya & pink grapefruit salad (recipe page 85)

lamb with heirloom tomato and almond salad
(recipe page 88)

Nutritional
COUNT PER SERVING

▸ 23.4g total fat
▸ 6.8g saturated fat
▸ 1805kJ (431 cal)
▸ 30.4g carbohydrate
▸ 21.3g protein
▸ 5.4g fibre
▸ 111mg sodium
▸ low GI

lamb with heirloom tomato and almond salad

PREP + COOK TIME 15 MINUTES • SERVES 2

½ cup (110g) risoni pasta

4 french-trimmed lamb cutlets (200g)

1 clove garlic, crushed

2 teaspoons finely chopped fresh rosemary leaves

2 teaspoons extra virgin olive oil

400g (12½ ounces) heirloom tomatoes, sliced

2 tablespoons flaked almonds, toasted

½ cup loosely packed fresh basil leaves

40g (1½ ounce) buffalo mozzarella, torn

1 tablespoon red wine vinegar

2 teaspoons extra virgin olive oil, extra

1 Cook pasta in a large saucepan of boiling water until tender; drain.

2 Meanwhile, combine lamb with garlic, rosemary and oil in a medium bowl. Cook lamb on a heated grill plate (or grill or barbecue) for 2 minutes each side or until cooked as desired.

3 Toss pasta with tomato, nuts, basil and cheese in a large bowl. Drizzle with vinegar and extra oil. Serve salad topped with lamb.

If you can't find buffalo mozzarella, use bocconcini.

(photograph page 87)

baked chicken with maple parsnips

PREP + COOK TIME 35 MINUTES • SERVES 2

2 teaspoons rice bran oil

2 x 200g (6½ ounce) skinless chicken thigh cutlets

3 small parsnips (360g), chopped coarsely

1 medium brown onion (150g), cut into wedges

2 cloves garlic, sliced

2 sprigs fresh rosemary

1 tablespoon maple syrup

¼ cup (60ml) salt-reduced chicken stock

¼ cup (60ml) water

4 medium trimmed silver beet leaves (swiss chard) (140g)

1 Heat oil in a heavy-based saucepan over high heat; cook chicken for 2 minutes each side or until browned. Remove from pan; cover to keep warm.

2 Reduce heat to medium. Add parsnip, onion, garlic and rosemary to pan; cook for 5 minutes or until browned. Return chicken to pan with maple syrup, stock and the water. Bring to the boil; cover, reduce heat to low. Simmer for 15 minutes or until chicken is just cooked through. Stir in silver beet; cook for 2 minutes or until wilted.

You could also use baby potatoes or carrots instead of the parsnips.

baked chicken with maple parsnips (recipe opposite)

Test Kitchen
NOTES

Raw buckwheat can be substituted for cracked buckwheat; simply blend or process the same amount of raw buckwheat until coarsely chopped. Remove any air from the cooked pizza base by gently pushing it down with a clean tea towel.

Nutritional
COUNT PER SERVING

- ▶ 11.9g total fat
- ▶ 2g saturated fat
- ▶ 1823kJ (435 cal)
- ▶ 45.5g carbohydrate
- ▶ 32.5g protein
- ▶ 6.5g fibre
- ▶ 429mg sodium
- ▶ medium GI

wholegrain pizza marinara

PREP + COOK TIME 45 MINUTES (+ REFRIGERATION & STANDING) • SERVES 2

1 fresh long red chilli, chopped finely

1 clove garlic, crushed

1 teaspoon finely grated lemon rind

1 tablespoon coarsely chopped fresh flat-leaf parsley

1 tablespoon rice bran oil

4 peeled medium king prawns (shrimp) (90g)

2 whole cleaned baby octopus (180g), halved lengthways

100g (3 ounces) cherry tomatoes, halved

25g (1 ounce) baby rocket leaves (arugula)

1 tablespoon fresh flat-leaf parsley leaves, extra

2 teaspoons lemon juice

DOUGH

1½ tablespoons cracked buckwheat

boiling water, to cover buckwheat

¼ cup (60ml) warm water

¼ teaspoon caster (superfine) sugar

½ teaspoon dried yeast

⅓ cup (55g) plain (all-purpose) flour

⅓ cup (60g) wholemeal plain (all-purpose) flour

1 Combine chilli, garlic, rind, parsley and oil in a small bowl, season with black pepper to taste. Divide garlic mixture in half; refrigerate one half of the mixture, covered. Combine remaining garlic mixture with prawns and octopus. Cover, refrigerate for 1 hour or overnight.

2 Make dough.

3 Meanwhile, preheat oven to 220°C/425°F. Lightly grease two large oven trays.

4 Bake pizza rounds for 8 minutes or until bases are partially cooked. Top with seafood mixture and tomato. Bake pizzas for a further 10 minutes or until bases are crisp and seafood is just cooked, drizzle with reserved garlic mixture.

5 Combine rocket, parsley and juice in a small bowl; season with pepper to taste.

6 Top pizzas with rocket mixture; serve immediately.

DOUGH Place buckwheat in a small heatproof bowl; cover with boiling water. Stand, covered for 30 minutes. Rinse under cold water; drain. Combine the warm water, sugar and yeast in a small jug, cover; stand in a warm place for 10 minutes or until frothy. Combine buckwheat and sifted flours in a medium bowl. Add yeast mixture; mix to a soft dough. Knead dough on a floured surface for 5 minutes or until smooth and elastic. Place dough in an oiled medium bowl. Cover; stand in a warm place for 45 minutes or until doubled in size. Halve dough. Roll each half into 15cm (6-inch) rounds; place on trays.

mushroom brown rice risotto

PREP + COOK TIME 1½ HOURS • SERVES 2

20g (½ ounce) dried porcini or mixed mushrooms

1.625 litres (6½ cups) water

½ cup (125ml) water, extra

1 small leek (200g), sliced thinly

1 clove garlic, crushed

⅔ cup (130g) doongara low-GI brown rice

2 tablespoons finely grated pecorino cheese

2 teaspoons rice bran oil

75g (2 ounces) oyster mushrooms, sliced thinly

75g (2 ounces) swiss brown mushrooms, sliced thinly

½ teaspoon finely chopped fresh thyme

1 teaspoon lemon juice

1 teaspoon fresh thyme leaves, extra

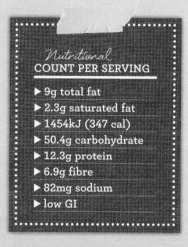

Nutritional
COUNT PER SERVING

▶ 9g total fat

▶ 2.3g saturated fat

▶ 1454kJ (347 cal)

▶ 50.4g carbohydrate

▶ 12.3g protein

▶ 6.9g fibre

▶ 82mg sodium

▶ low GI

1 Combine dried mushrooms and the water in a medium saucepan over medium heat, bring to a simmer. Remove from heat; stand for 15 minutes. Drain broth into a clean saucepan; reserve broth. Finely chop 2 teaspoons mushrooms, discard the remaining mushrooms. Return broth to heat; simmer, covered, over low heat.

2 Combine the extra water, leek and garlic in a medium saucepan over medium heat; cook, stirring occasionally, for 10 minutes or until leek is tender, (add an extra 1 tablespoon of water at a time if the pan becomes dry).

3 Add rice and reserved mushrooms to the pan, stirring to combine. Add 1 cup hot broth mixture; cook, stirring occasionally, over low heat, until broth is absorbed. Continue adding broth mixture, in 1-cup batches, stirring until absorbed between additions. Total cooking time should be approximately 50 minutes or until rice is tender. Stir half the cheese into the risotto.

4 Heat oil in a medium non-stick frying pan over high heat. Add oyster and swiss brown mushrooms and chopped thyme; cook, stirring occasionally, for 5 minutes or until mushrooms are browned lightly. Stir in juice, season with black pepper. Remove from heat; cover to keep warm.

5 Serve risotto topped with mushrooms, thyme leaves and remaining cheese.

You could also use a combination of button and enoki mushrooms in this risotto.

pork and tofu rice noodles

Nutritional
COUNT PER SERVING

▶ 14.4g total fat
▶ 2.4g saturated fat
▶ 1797kJ (429 cal)
▶ 34.4g carbohydrate
▶ 34.4g protein
▶ 10.5g fibre
▶ 414mg sodium
▶ medium GI

125g (4 ounces) rice stick noodles

3 teaspoons rice bran oil

150g (4½ ounces) lean pork fillet, sliced thinly

150g (4 ½ ounces) firm tofu, drained, cut into 2.5cm (1-inch) cubes

2 cloves garlic, crushed

1 fresh small red thai (serrano) chilli, sliced thinly

1 small red onion (100g), cut into thin wedges

1 tablespoon water

1 medium yellow capsicum (bell pepper) (200g), sliced thinly

150g (4½ ounces) green beans, halved diagonally

150g (4½ ounces) oyster mushrooms, halved if large

2 tablespoons water, extra

1 tablespoon salt-reduced soy sauce

¼ cup loosely packed fresh coriander leaves (cilantro)

1 Place noodles in a medium heatproof bowl, cover with boiling water; stand until just tender, drain.
2 Meanwhile, heat 2 teaspoons of the oil in a wok over high heat; stir-fry pork for 3 minutes or until browned. Remove from wok; cover to keep warm.
3 Heat the remaining oil in wok over medium-high heat; stir-fry tofu, garlic, chilli, onion and the water for 3 minutes or until onion starts to soften. Add capsicum, beans and mushrooms to wok; stir-fry for 2 minutes. Add the extra water; stir-fry for 1 minute or until vegetables are just tender. Add sauce, pork and noodles; stir-fry until heated through.
4 Serve stir-fry topped with coriander.

To make this recipe gluten-free, swap the soy sauce for 2 teaspoons of gluten-free tamari.

grilled pork with quinoa and kale salad

PREP + COOK TIME 30 MINUTES • SERVES 2

⅓ cup (70g) black quinoa

1 small zucchini (90g), sliced into ribbons

1 medium carrot (120g), sliced into ribbons

1 small clove garlic, crushed

2 tablespoons lemon juice

1 tablespoon rice bran oil

2 x 125g (4 ounce) pork medallions

50g (1½ ounces) baby kale

1 tablespoon fresh mint leaves

2 teaspoons pine nuts, toasted

½ lemon (70g), cut into wedges

1 Rinse and drain quinoa well. Cook quinoa in a small saucepan of boiling water for 10 minutes or until tender; drain. Refresh under cold water; drain.
2 Meanwhile, place zucchini, carrot, garlic, juice and half the oil in a medium bowl; toss gently to combine.
3 Heat remaining oil in a small frying pan over high heat; cook pork for 3 minutes each side or until browned both sides and just cooked through.
4 Add quinoa, kale, mint and nuts to zucchini mixture; toss gently to combine.
5 Serve pork with salad and lemon wedges.

Nutritional
COUNT PER SERVING

▶ 16.4g total fat
▶ 2.6g saturated fat
▶ 1737kJ (415 cal)
▶ 27.6g carbohydrate
▶ 35.8g protein
▶ 6.2g fibre
▶ 116mg sodium
▶ low GI

BROWN RICE

baby carrot & spinach pilaf
PREP + COOK TIME 45 MINUTES • SERVES 2

Heat 2 teaspoons of olive oil in a medium saucepan over medium-high heat; cook 6 halved baby carrots for 5 minutes or until browned. Remove from pan. Cook half a finely chopped small brown onion in same pan, stirring, for 3 minutes or until softened. Stir in ¾ cup low-GI doongara brown rice and 1½ cups water; bring to the boil. Reduce heat; simmer, covered, for 25 minutes or until the rice is tender, returning carrots to the pan for the last 10 minutes of cooking time. Stir in 40g (1½ ounces) baby spinach leaves and 1 tablespoon small fresh mint leaves.

▶ **nutritional count per serving** 6.9g total fat (1.2g saturated fat); 1395kJ (333 cal); 57.3g carbohydrate; 7.3g protein; 5.4g fibre; 29mg sodium; low GI

kumara & rocket pilaf
PREP + COOK TIME 45 MINUTES • SERVES 2

Heat 2 teaspoons of olive oil in a medium saucepan over a medium-high heat; cook 150g (4½ ounces) coarsely chopped kumara (orange sweet potato) and half a finely chopped small brown onion, stirring, for 5 minutes or until onion softens. Stir in ⅔ cup low-GI doongara brown rice and 1⅓ cups water; bring to the boil. Reduce heat to low, cover; simmer, for 25 minutes or until the rice is tender. Stir in 30g (1 ounce) baby rocket leaves (arugula) and 1 tablespoon toasted pepitas.

▶ **nutritional count per serving** 9.4g total fat (1.5g saturated fat); 1615kJ (386 cal); 63g carbohydrate; 9.3g protein; 5.3g fibre; 18mg sodium; low GI

brown fried rice

PREP + COOK TIME 45 MINUTES • SERVES 2

Cook ⅔ cup low-GI doongara brown rice in a large
pan of boiling water for 25 minutes or until tender;
drain. Heat 2 teaspoons of peanut oil in a large wok
over a medium-high heat; swirl 1 lightly beaten egg
to coat base of pan, cook for 1 minute or until just
set. Transfer to a plate; slice egg thinly. Heat
2 teaspoons peanut oil in wok over medium-high
heat; stir-fry 2 cups fresh or frozen stir-fry vegetable
mix and 2 tablespoons water for 5 minutes or until
just tender. Add rice to wok with 2 teaspoons kecap
manis; stir to combine. Stir in egg and ⅓ cup fresh
coriander leaves (cilantro). Serve fried rice topped
with sliced fresh long red chilli, if you like.

▶ **nutritional count per serving** 10.9g total fat
(2.7g saturated fat); 1744kJ (417 cal); 59.6g carbohydrate;
12.9g protein; 13.8g fibre; 447mg sodium; low GI

greek brown rice salad

PREP + COOK TIME 50 MINUTES • SERVES 2

Place ¾ cup low-GI long grain brown rice and
1½ cups water in a small saucepan; bring to the
boil, then simmer, covered, for 25 minutes or
until tender. Remove from heat; stand, covered,
for 5 minutes. Add 6 pitted halved black olives,
1 chopped lebanese cucumber, ½ chopped small
avocado, 1 cup halved cherry tomatoes, ½ thinly
sliced small red onion and 2 tablespoons each fresh
oregano and basil leaves. Combine 2 tablespoons
red wine vinegar, 3 teaspoons rice bran oil and
1 crushed garlic clove; pour dressing over salad,
toss to combine.

▶ **nutritional count per serving** 19.3g total fat
(3.5g saturated fat); 1942kJ (464 cal); 59.2g carbohydrate;
8.5g protein; 7.2g fibre; 211mg sodium; low GI

sweets

tropical jelly with coconut yoghurt

PREP + COOK TIME 10 MINUTES (+ REFRIGERATION) • SERVES 2

1 x 9g (½ ounce) sachet sugar-free mango and passionfruit jelly crystals

1 cup (250ml) boiling water

1 cup (250ml) cold water

1 small mango (300g), sliced

2 tablespoons coconut yoghurt

2 tablespoons fresh passionfruit pulp

1 tablespoon fresh mint leaves

1 Place jelly and the boiling water in a medium bowl. Stir to dissolve crystals. Add the cold water; stir to combine.

2 Divide mango between two 1½-cup (375ml) glasses; pour over jelly. Refrigerate for at least 4 hours or until set.

3 Top jellies with yoghurt, passionfruit and mint.

You can make these jellies the day ahead, just cover with plastic wrap and refrigerate. Top with yoghurt, passionfruit and mint just before serving.

roasted pears with cinnamon labneh (recipe opposite)

roasted pears with cinnamon labneh

PREP + COOK TIME 1 HOUR (+ REFRIGERATION) • SERVES 2

Start this recipe a day ahead.

½ cup (140g) low-fat greek yoghurt

1 herbal lemon tea bag

1 cup (250ml) boiling water

2 strips lemon rind

1 teaspoon honey

2 small firm pears (360gg), peeled, halved, cored

¼ teaspoon ground cinnamon

2 teaspoons chopped roasted hazelnuts

1 Line a sieve or colander with muslin, place over a large bowl. Spoon yoghurt into muslin; cover with plastic wrap. Refrigerate overnight to drain; discard any liquid.
2 Preheat oven to 200°C/400°F.
3 Combine tea bag, the boiling water, rind and half the honey in a small bowl. Stand for 5 minutes. Drain; discard tea bag.
4 Place pears in a medium baking dish; pour over tea mixture. Transfer to oven; roast for 45 minutes, turning every 15 minutes, or until pears are tender.
5 Combine yoghurt, cinnamon and remaining honey in a small bowl.
6 Serve pears with yoghurt mixture; drizzle with any cooking liquid and sprinkle with nuts.

Use a melon baller to core the pears. You can use bought labneh in this recipe if you are time poor, just be aware the nutritional count will change; make sure you check the label for the sodium and fat content.

rhubarb and vanilla baked custard

PREP + COOK TIME 50 MINUTES • SERVES 2

4 stems trimmed rhubarb (250g), chopped coarsely

2 tablespoons caster (superfine) sugar

1 vanilla bean, split lengthways

2 small eggs

1 cup (250ml) hot low-fat milk

pinch ground nutmeg

1 Preheat oven to 220°C/425°F. Grease and line a large baking tray. Grease two 1½-cup (375ml) ovenproof dishes.
2 Toss rhubarb with 2 teaspoons of the sugar on baking tray. Roast for 15 minutes or until rhubarb is tender. Mash rhubarb with a fork. Divide rhubarb between ovenproof dishes. Reduce oven temperature to 160°C/325°F.
3 Remove seeds from vanilla bean. Whisk eggs, vanilla seeds and remaining sugar in a medium bowl; whisk in hot milk. Gently pour custard mixture over rhubarb in dishes; sprinkle with nutmeg.
4 Place dishes in a medium baking dish; add enough boiling water to come halfway up side of dishes. Bake for 30 minutes or until custard is just set.

The rhubarb can be made up to 3 days in advance; store, covered, in the fridge. Place the empty vanilla pod in a jar then cover it with caster sugar to make your own vanilla sugar.

(photograph page 102)

rhubarb and vanilla baked custard (recipe page 101)

Nutritional
COUNT PER SERVING

▶ 4.3g total fat
▶ 1.5g saturated fat
▶ 761kJ (181 cal)
▶ 30g carbohydrate
▶ 4.6g protein
▶ 2.6g fibre
▶ 139mg sodium
▶ low GI

nectarine and almond tarte tartin (recipe page 104)

nectarine and almond tarte tartin

PREP + COOK TIME 50 MINUTES · SERVES 2

5g (¼ ounce) butter

1 tablespoon water

2 tablespoons brown sugar

1 vanilla bean, split lengthways, seeds removed

2 medium nectarines (340g), halved, seeded, cut into thin wedges

1 tablespoon slivered almonds

2 sheets fillo pastry

1 teaspoon skim milk

2 tablespoons fat-free natural yoghurt

1 Preheat oven to 200°C/400°F.
2 Combine butter, the water, sugar and vanilla bean pod and seeds in a small ovenproof frying pan over medium heat; cook, stirring, for 1 minute or until butter has melted and sugar has dissolved.
3 Increase heat to high, add nectarines and nuts; cook, stirring, for 2 minutes or until liquid has thickened slightly. Remove vanilla pod.
4 Meanwhile, brush each pastry sheet on one side with milk, place one pastry sheet on top of the other, brushed-side up; place over nectarines in the pan and carefully tuck pastry in around the edges.
5 Bake for 20 minutes or until pastry is golden and crisp. Carefully turn onto a plate. Cut in half and serve with yoghurt.

(photograph page 103)

orange and pomegranate steamed puddings

PREP + COOK TIME 45 MINUTES · SERVES 2

2½ tablespoons brown sugar

½ medium orange (240g), segmented

1 small egg

2½ tablespoons wholemeal self-raising flour

1 tablespoon ground almonds

1 tablespoon orange juice

1 tablespoon fresh pomegranate

1 tablespoon low-fat custard

1 Grease and line base of 2 x ¾-cup (180ml) dariole moulds or ramekins with baking paper.
2 Sprinkle 2 teaspoons of the sugar on the base of the moulds; top with orange segments.
3 Beat remaining sugar and egg in a small bowl with an electric mixer for 2 minutes or until thick and creamy. Fold in remaining ingredients.
4 Divide mixture between moulds, cover with a layer of pleated foil and baking paper; secure with kitchen string.
5 Place puddings in a medium saucepan with enough boiling water to come halfway up the sides of moulds. Cover with a tight fitting lid; simmer for 25 minutes. Stand puddings for 5 minutes. Serve each pudding with 2 teaspoons of custard.

Puddings can be made a day ahead; reheat in microwave for 15 second bursts until heated through.

orange and pomegranate steamed puddings (recipe opposite)

4 Ways with
ICE CREAM

very berry
ice-cream sandwiches

PREP TIME 15 MINUTES (+ FREEZING) • SERVES 2

Combine ¼ cup (35g) mixed frozen berries in a
medium bowl. Stand for 10 minutes or until slightly
thawed; crush lightly. Stir in ½ cup 97% fat-free
no-added sugar vanilla ice-cream. Transfer
ice-cream to a freezer-proof container. Freeze for
1 hour or until firm. Sandwich scoops of ice-cream
between 4 breakfast biscuits.

▶ nutritional count per serving 4.3g total fat
(1.3g saturated fat); 660kJ (158 cal); 24.9g carbohydrate;
3.8g protein; 1.2g fibre; 125mg sodium; low GI

We used Belvita Breakfast biscuits. Allow ice-cream to
soften slightly before stirring in ingredients.

coconut & lime
ice-cream sandwiches

PREP TIME 10 MINUTES (+ FREEZING) • SERVES 2

Combine 2 teaspoons toasted shredded coconut,
1 teaspoon finely grated lime rind and ½ cup
97% fat-free no-added sugar vanilla ice-cream in a
medium bowl; stir to combine. Transfer ice-cream
to a freezer-proof container. Freeze for 1 hour or
until firm. Sandwich scoops of ice-cream between
4 breakfast biscuits.

▶ nutritional count per serving 5.2g total fat
(2.1g saturated fat); 684kJ (164 cal); 24.4g carbohydrate;
3.6g protein; 1.1g fibre; 124mg sodium; low GI

We used Belvita Breakfast biscuits. Allow ice-cream to
soften slightly before stirring in ingredients.

coffee & hazelnut ice-cream sandwiches

PREP TIME 15 MINUTES (+ FREEZING) • SERVES 2

Combine 1 teaspoon cold espresso coffee and 2 teaspoons finely chopped toasted hazelnuts in a medium bowl. Stir in ½ cup 97% fat-free no-added sugar vanilla ice-cream. Transfer ice-cream to a freezer-proof container. Freeze for 1 hour or until firm. Sandwich scoops of ice-cream between 4 breakfast biscuits.

▶ **nutritional count per serving** 4.9g total fat (1.3g saturated fat); 667kJ (160 cal); 24.3g carbohydrate; 3.6g protein; 0.9g fibre; 125mg sodium; low GI

We used Belvita Breakfast biscuits. Allow ice-cream to soften slightly before stirring in ingredients.

caramel swirl ice-cream sandwiches

PREP TIME 10 MINUTES (+ FREEZING) • SERVES 2

Place ½ cup 97% fat-free no-added sugar vanilla ice-cream in a freezer-proof container; gently swirl in 2 teaspoons caramel sauce. Freeze ice-cream for 1 hour or until firm. Sandwich scoops of ice-cream between 4 breakfast biscuits.

▶ **nutritional count per serving** 4.3g total fat (1.3g saturated fat); 719kJ (172 cal); 29g carbohydrate; 3.6g protein; 0.8g fibre; 149mg sodium; low GI

We used Belvita Breakfast biscuits. Allow ice-cream to soften slightly before stirring in ingredients.

fig and orange blossom rice pudding

PREP + COOK TIME 55 MINUTES (+ STANDING) • SERVES 2

¼ cup (50g) low-GI white rice

1 cup (250ml) skim milk

1 cinnamon stick

1 cardamom pod, bruised

1 small egg yolk

¼ teaspoon orange blossom water

2 teaspoons finely grated orange rind

1 fresh fig (60g), quartered

10 pistachios, chopped

2 teaspoons fresh mint leaves

2 teaspoons honey

1 Cook rice in a small saucepan of boiling water for 20 minutes or until soft. Drain well.

2 Meanwhile, heat milk, cinnamon and cardamom in a small non-stick saucepan over low heat. Bring just to a simmer, then remove from heat; cover and stand for 20 minutes to infuse.

3 Add rice to milk mixture; simmer over low heat for 10 minutes. Add egg yolk; stir over low heat for 30 seconds or until thickened slightly. Stir in orange blossom water and rind. Cool for 20 minutes or until mixture is warm. Discard cinnamon and cardamom.

4 Preheat grill (broiler) to high. Place figs on a foil-lined oven tray; grill for 3 minutes or until figs are browned and tender.

5 Spoon rice into 2 small serving glasses; top with figs and any juices, nuts and mint. Drizzle with honey.

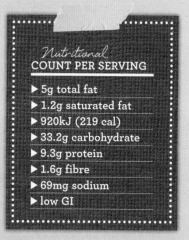

Nutritional
COUNT PER SERVING

▶ 5g total fat

▶ 1.2g saturated fat

▶ 920kJ (219 cal)

▶ 33.2g carbohydrate

▶ 9.3g protein

▶ 1.6g fibre

▶ 69mg sodium

▶ low GI

chocolate and ricotta crepes with spiced dates

PREP + COOK TIME 30 MINUTES (+ COOLING) • SERVES 2

2 fresh dates (40g), seeded, cut into slivers

½ cup (125ml) water

1 cinnamon stick

¼ teaspoon vanilla extract

1 teaspoon brown sugar

⅓ cup (50g) wholemeal plain (all-purpose) flour

⅔ cup (160ml) skim milk

1 small egg, beaten lightly

rice bran oil spray

¼ cup (60g) low-fat fresh ricotta

1 tablespoon finely grated dark chocolate (85% cocoa)

1 Combine dates, the water, cinnamon, extract and sugar in a small saucepan over low heat; bring to the boil. Reduce heat to low, simmer, uncovered, for 10 minutes or until liquid is reduced to 2 tablespoons. Cool.

2 Place flour in a medium bowl; gradually whisk in combined milk and egg until smooth. Stand for 10 minutes.

3 Spray a small non-stick crêpe or frying pan with a little oil spray. Heat pan over medium heat; add ¼ cup crêpe mixture to pan, swirling to make to a thin layer. Cook for 30 seconds each side or until golden. Transfer to a plate. Repeat with remaining mixture to make a total of 4 crêpes.

4 Combine ricotta and 3 teaspoons of the chocolate in a small bowl. Divide the ricotta mixture into the centre of two crêpes; fold up to form parcels. Serve topped with dates, syrup and remaining chocolate.

Test Kitchen
NOTES

If serving more than two people make double the amount of the date syrup and chocolate ricotta mixtures. The dates will weigh about 27g (¾ ounce) once the seeds are removed.

You only need one crêpe per serve for this recipe. Freeze the remaining two crêpes for up to three months.

Cooking TECHNIQUES

preparing asparagus

To snap the woody end off the asparagus, hold it close to the base and bend it until it snaps. Discard the woody end and then trim the asparagus with a vegetable peeler.

crushing garlic

Press garlic firmly with the flat blade of a large knife (top) crushing the clove. Simply pull off the papery skin. A garlic press (bottom) removes and leaves the skin behind while crushing the garlic.

trimming beetroot

To trim beetroot, cut the stems to 2cm (¾ inch) from the bulb. Don't trim the beard at the base of the plant as this stops the colour from bleeding during cooking.

removing corn kernels

Remove the husk (the outer covering) and the silk (the soft silky inner threads), and trim one side of the corn cob so it lies flat. Use a large flat-bladed knife to cut down the cob, close to the core, to remove the kernels.

slicing vegies thinly

Cutting cucumber, zucchini, carrots, etc, into thin ribbons gives long thin, uniform slices. Use a vegetable peeler to do this. Applying more pressure on the peeler gives a thicker slice.

trimming watercress

Use scissors to cut off the roots, then pull the leaves off any thick, woody stems. This peppery green may also be known as 'winter rocket'.

how to chiffonade

Chiffonade is a way of cutting green leaves into long, thin strips. Lay leaves flat on top of each other, then roll up tightly and cut into thin slices.

trimming a green onion

Pull the papery skin towards the root and off the onion. Cut the root end off, then slice the white end of the onion as directed in the recipe. The green end can be used to garnish the dish.

making a thin omelette

To make a thin omelette, lightly whisk the eggs, then pour into a heated lightly-oiled wok (or large frying pan). Tilt the wok to cover the base with the egg; cook until the egg is set.

slicing a chilli

When slicing a chilli, leave it whole. The seeds are the heat source, so if you are intolerant of high heat levels, remove the seeds and membranes, or use less chilli. Don't touch your face after touching chilli as it can burn your eyes and mouth.

slicing fennel

Slicing fennel thinly is easy using a V-slicer or mandoline – simply slide the fennel back and forth across the blade. The adjustable blade is very sharp, so watch your fingers. A guard is supplied, so use it to protect your fingers from any unwanted mishaps.

slicing capsicum

To slice a capsicum, cut the top and bottom off and stand it on one end; slice down removing all the flesh. Remove and discard the seeds and membranes, then slice the flesh.

GLOSSARY

ALL-BRAN CEREAL a low-fat, high-fibre breakfast cereal based on wheat bran.

BAKING POWDER a raising agent consisting mainly of two parts cream of tartar to one part bicarbonate of soda (baking soda).

BASIL an aromatic herb; there are many types, but the most commonly used is sweet, or common, basil.
thai also known as horapa; different from holy basil and sweet basil in both look and taste, having smaller leaves and purplish stems. It has a slight aniseed taste and is one of the identifying flavours of Thai food.

BEANS
black also known as turtle beans or black kidney beans; an earthy-flavoured bean completely different from the better-known chinese black beans (which are fermented soya beans).
broad also known as fava, windsor and horse beans. Fresh and frozen forms should be peeled twice (discarding both the outer long green pod and the beige-green tough inner shell).
cannellini small white bean similar in appearance and flavour to great northern, navy and haricot beans – all of which can be substituted for the other. Available dried or canned.
kidney medium-sized red bean, slightly floury in texture yet sweet in flavour; sold dried or canned.
sprouts also known as bean shoots; tender new growths of assorted beans and seeds grown for consumption as sprouts. The most readily available are mung bean, soya bean, alfalfa and snow pea sprouts.
white in this book, some recipes may call for 'white beans', a generic term we use for cannellini, great northern, haricot or navy beans, all of which can be substituted for the other.

BICARBONATE OF SODA also known as baking or carb soda; is used as a leavening agent in baking.

BUK CHOY also known as bok choy, pak choi, chinese white cabbage or chinese chard; has a fresh, mild mustard taste. Baby buk choy, also known as pak kat farang or shanghai bok choy, is much smaller and more tender than buk choy.

BUTTERMILK originally the term given to the slightly sour liquid left after butter was churned from cream, today it is made similarly to yogurt. Sold alongside all fresh milk products in supermarkets; despite the implication of its name, it is low in fat.

CAVOLO NERO also known as tuscan cabbage or tuscan black cabbage. It has long, narrow, wrinkled leaves and a rich and astringent, mild cabbage flavour. It doesn't lose its volume like silver beet or spinach when cooked, but it does need longer cooking. It is a member of the kale family; if you can't find it use silver beet (swiss chard) or cabbage instead.

CHEESE
cottage fresh, white, unripened curd cheese with a grainy consistency and a fat content between 5% and 15%.
cream commonly known as Philly or Philadelphia, a soft cows'-milk cheese with a fat content of at least 33%. Also available as spreadable light cream cheese, a blend of cottage and cream cheeses with a fat content of 21%.
goat made from goats' milk, has an earthy, strong taste; available in soft and firm textures, in various shapes and sizes, and sometimes rolled in ash or herbs.
mozzarella a soft, spun-curd cheese. It has a low melting point and an elastic texture when heated; used to add texture rather than flavour. A favourite cheese for pizza.
parmesan also known as parmigiano, parmesan is a hard, grainy cows'-milk cheese. The curd is salted in brine for a month before being aged for up to two years in humid conditions.

ricotta the name for this soft, white, cows'-milk cheese roughly translates as 'cooked again'. It's made from whey, a by-product of other cheese-making, to which fresh milk and acid are added.
tasty a matured cheddar; use an aged, strongly-flavoured, hard variety.

CHICKPEAS also called garbanzos, hummus or channa; an irregularly round, sandy-coloured legume.

CHILLI available in many different types and sizes. Use rubber gloves when seeding and chopping fresh chillies as they can burn your skin. Removing seeds and membranes lessens the heat level.
flakes, dried deep-red, dehydrated chilli slices and whole seeds.
long green or red available both fresh and dried; a generic term used for any moderately hot, long (about 6cm to 8cm), thin chilli.
red thai also known as 'scuds'; small, very hot and bright red in colour.

CHINESE FIVE-SPICE POWDER a fragrant mixture of ground cinnamon, cloves, star anise, sichuan pepper and fennel seeds.

CHOY SUM also known as pakaukeo or flowering cabbage, a member of the buk choy family; easy to identify with its long stems, light green leaves and yellow flowers. Is eaten, stems and all, steamed or stir-fried.

CORIANDER also known as pak chee, cilantro or chinese parsley; bright-green leafy herb with a pungent flavour. Both the stems and roots of coriander are used; wash well before using. Is also available ground or as seeds; these should not be substituted for fresh as the tastes are completely different.

CORNFLOUR also known as cornstarch; used as a thickening agent in cooking. Wheaten cornflour is made from wheat rather than corn and gives cakes a lighter texture (due to the fact wheaten cornflour has some gluten).

CREAM we used fresh cream, also known as pouring or pure cream, unless otherwise stated. It has no additives unlike thickened cream. Minimum fat content 35%.

sour a thick, cultured soured cream. Minimum fat content 35%.

thickened a whipping cream containing a thickener. Minimum fat content 35%.

DAIKON also known as giant white radish. Used extensively in Japanese cooking; has a sweet, fresh flavour without the bite of the common red radish.

FENNEL also known as finocchio or anise; a white to very pale green-white, firm, crisp, roundish vegetable about 8cm-12cm in diameter. The bulb has a slightly sweet, anise flavour but the leaves have a much stronger taste. Also the name given to dried seeds having a licorice flavour.

FLAT-LEAF PARSLEY also known as continental parsley or italian parsley.

FLOUR

buckwheat a herb in the same plant family as rhubarb; not a cereal so it is gluten-free.

plain a general all-purpose flour made from wheat.

rice a very fine flour, made from ground white rice.

self-raising plain flour sifted with baking powder in the proportion of 1 cup flour to 2 teaspoons baking powder. Also called self-rising flour.

spelt very similar to wheat, but has a slightly nuttier, sweeter flavour. Spelt flour contains gluten.

wholemeal milled from whole wheat grain (bran, germ and endosperm).

GAI LAN also known as chinese broccoli, gai larn, kanah, gai lum, chinese broccoli and chinese kale; appreciated more for its stems than its coarse leaves.

GINGER, FRESH also known as green or root ginger; the thick root of a tropical plant.

HARISSA a hot Moroccan sauce or paste made from dried chillies, cumin, garlic, oil and caraway seeds. The paste, available in a tube, is very hot and should not be used in large amounts; bottled harissa sauce is milder, but is still hot. If you have a low heat-level tolerance, you may find any recipe containing harissa too hot to tolerate. Available from supermarkets and Middle-Eastern grocery stores.

KAFFIR LIME LEAVES also known as bai magrood, look like two glossy dark green leaves joined end to end, forming a rounded hourglass shape. Used similarly to bay leaves or curry leaves. Sold fresh, dried or frozen; dried leaves are less potent so double the number if using them as a substitute for fresh. A strip of fresh lime peel may be substituted for each kaffir lime leaf.

MISO Japan's famous bean paste made from fermented soya beans and rice, rye or barley. It varies in colour, texture and saltiness. White miso tends to have a sweeter and somewhat less salty flavour than the darker red miso. Brown miso has a very strong flavour. Dissolve miso in a little water before adding. Keeps well refrigerated.

MOUNTAIN BREAD a thin, dry, soft-textured bread, that can be rolled up and filled with your favourite filling.

MUSHROOM

cup a common white mushroom picked just as the veil, or underside, begins to open around the stem. Has a full-bodied flavour and firm texture.

enoki clumps of long, spaghetti-like stems with tiny, snowy white caps.

flat large, flat mushrooms with a rich earthy flavour. They are sometimes misnamed field mushrooms, which are wild mushrooms.

porcini, dried the richest flavoured mushrooms; also known as cèpes. Have a strong nutty flavour, so only small amounts are required. Must be rehydrated before use.

shiitake when fresh are also known as chinese black, forest or golden oak mushrooms; although cultivated, they have the earthiness and taste of wild mushrooms. Are large and meaty.

swiss brown also called roman or cremini; are light-to-dark brown in colour with a full-bodied flavour.

OIL, GRAPE SEED is a good-quality, neutral vegetable oil pressed from grape seeds.

PAPRIKA a ground dried sweet red capsicum (bell pepper); there are many grades and types available, including sweet, hot, mild and smoked.

PINE NUTS also known as pignoli; not in fact a nut but a small, cream-coloured kernel from pine cones.

PITTA BREAD also known as lebanese bread. This wheat-flour pocket bread is sold in large, flat pieces that separate into two thin rounds. Also available in small thick pieces called pocket pitta.

POMEGRANATE a dark-red, leathery-skinned fruit about the size of an orange filled with hundreds of seeds, each wrapped in an edible lucent-crimson pulp having a tangy sweet-sour flavour. *To remove pomegranate seeds*, cut the pomegranate in half, and use gloved fingers to scrape the seeds from the flesh whilst holding the pomegranate upside down in a bowl of cold water; the seeds will sink and the white pith will float to the surface. Discard the pith, and drain the seeds before using.

pomegranate molasses a thick, tangy syrup made by boiling pomegranate juice into a sticky, syrupy consistency. Available from Middle Eastern food stores, specialty food shops and delis.

POTATO, BABY NEW also known as chats; not a separate variety but an early harvest with very thin skin.

PROSCIUTTO a thinly-sliced Italian, dry-cured ham. Available as crudo (raw) and cotto (cooked).

MAPLE SYRUP a thin syrup distilled from the sap of the maple tree. Maple-flavoured or pancake syrup is not an adequate substitute for the real thing.

QUINOA (keen-wa) the seed of a leafy plant similar to spinach. It has a delicate, slightly nutty taste and chewy texture. Its cooking qualities are similar to that of rice. You can buy it in most health-food stores; it spoils easily, so keep it sealed in a glass jar in the fridge. *Quinoa flakes* are rolled and flattened grains.

RADISH, RED a peppery root vegetable related to the mustard plant. The small round red variety is the mildest, it is crisp and juicy, and usually eaten raw in salads.

RHUBARB has thick, celery-like stalks that can reach up to 60cm long; the stalks are the only edible portion of the plant – the leaves contain a toxic substance.

RICE
basmati a white, fragrant long-grained rice. Wash well before cooking.
brown basmati has more fibre and a stronger flavour than white basmati, but it takes twice as long to cook.
microwave milled, cooked then dried rice. Pre-cooked rice is more porous, so that steam can penetrate the grain and rehydrate it in a short time.

RICE NOODLES, DRIED made from rice flour and water, available flat and wide or very thin (vermicelli). Should be soaked in boiling water to soften. Also known as rice stick noodles.

RISONI a small, rice-shaped pasta.

ROLLED OATS oat groats (oats that have been husked) steamed-softened, flattened with rollers, then dried and packaged for consumption as a cereal.

SASHIMI GRADE SALMON use the freshest, sashimi-quality fish you can find. Raw fish sold as sashimi has to meet stringent guidelines regarding its handling and treatment after leaving the water. Seek local advice from authorities before eating any raw seafood.

SAUCE
fish also called nam pla or nuoc nam; made from pulverised fermented fish, most often anchovies. Has a pungent smell and strong taste; use sparingly.
hoisin a thick, sweet and spicy chinese paste made from salted fermented soya beans, onions and garlic.
oyster Asian in origin, this rich, brown sauce is made from oysters and their brine, cooked with salt and soy sauce, and thickened with starches.
soy also known as sieu, is made from fermented soya beans. Several variations are available in most supermarkets and Asian food stores.
sweet chilli a comparatively mild, thai-type sauce made from red chillies, sugar, garlic and vinegar.

SEMOLINA made from durum (hard) wheat milled into textured granules.

SHALLOT also called french shallots, golden shallots or eschalots; small, elongated, brown-skinned members of the onion family. Grows in tight clusters similar to garlic.

SNOW PEAS also called mange tout (eat all). *Snow pea tendrils*, the growing shoots of the plant, are sold by greengrocers. *Snow pea sprouts* tender new growths of snow peas; also known as mange tout.

SUGAR
brown a soft, finely granulated sugar retaining molasses for its characteristic colour and flavour.
caster also known as superfine or finely granulated table sugar.
icing also known as confectioners' sugar or powdered sugar; granulated sugar crushed together with a small amount of added cornflour.
low-GI cane a molasses extract is sprayed onto raw sugar, increasing the time it takes to digest the sugar, resulting in a slower release of energy.

SULTANAS dried grapes, also known as golden raisins.

SUMAC a purple-red, astringent spice ground from berries grown on shrubs that flourish around the Mediterranean; adds a tart, lemony flavour to foods.

TAHINI sesame-seed paste.

TOFU also known as bean curd, an off-white, custard-like product made from the 'milk' of crushed soya beans; comes fresh (soft or firm), or processed (fried or pressed dried sheets). Left over fresh tofu can be refrigerated in water (which is changed daily) for up to 4 days.
silken refers to the method by which it is made – strained through silk.

TOMATOES
roma (egg) also called plum, these are the smallish, oval-shaped tomatoes used in Italian cooking.
truss also known as tiny tim or tom thumb tomatoes; vine-ripened tomatoes with the vine still attached.

TURMERIC a member of the ginger family, its root is dried and ground, resulting in the rich yellow powder that gives many Indian dishes their characteristic colour. It is intensely pungent in taste, but not hot.

VANILLA
bean dried long, thin pod from a tropical golden orchid; the tiny black seeds are used to impart a luscious vanilla flavour.
extract made by pulping chopped vanilla beans with a mixture of alcohol and water. This gives a very strong solution, and only a couple of drops are needed.

VINEGAR
balsamic made from Trebbiano grapes; has a deep rich brown colour with a sweet and sour flavour.
red wine based on fermented red wine.

WASABI an Asian horseradish used to make the pungent, green-coloured sauce traditionally served with Japanese raw fish dishes; sold in powdered or paste form.

ZUCCHINI also known as courgette; small green, yellow or white vegetable belonging to the squash family.

INDEX

This book is published in 2015 by Octopus Publishing Group Limited
based on materials licensed to it by Bauer Media Books, Australia

Bauer Media Books is a division of Bauer Media Pty Limited.

54 Park St, Sydney; GPO Box 4088, Sydney, NSW 2001, Australia

phone (+61) 2 9282 8618; fax (+61) 2 9126 3702

www.awwcookbooks.com.au

MEDIA GROUP

BAUER MEDIA BOOKS

Publisher – Jo Runciman

Editorial & food director – Pamela Clark

Director of sales, marketing & rights – Brian Cearnes

Art director & designer – Hannah Blackmore

Senior editor – Wendy Bryant

Food editor – Emma Braz

Published and Distributed in the United Kingdom by Octopus Publishing Group

Endeavour House

189 Shaftesbury Avenue

London WC2H 8JY

phone (+44) (0) 207 632 5400; fax (+44) (0) 207 632 5405

info@octopus-publishing.co.uk;

www.octopusbooks.co.uk

Printed by Toppan Printing Co, Hong Kong

International foreign language rights, Brian Cearnes, Bauer Media Books bcearnes@bauer-media.com.au

A catalogue record for this book is available from the British Library.
ISBN: 978 1909770 28 7 (paperback)

© Bauer Media Pty Ltd 2015
ABN 18 053 273 546

THE AUSTRALIAN Women's Weekly

ALSO FROM THE BEST-SELLING COOKERY SERIES OF ALL TIME

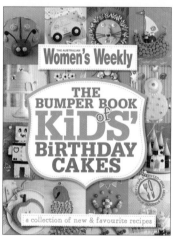

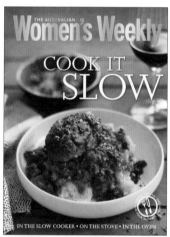

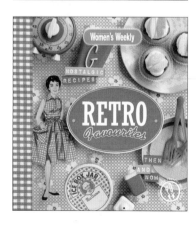

To order books visit www.octopusbooks.co.uk or telephone +44 (0)1903 828 503